Legal Issues and Guidelines
For Nurses Who Care For The Mentally Ill

JOYCE KEMP LABEN RN, MSN, JD

COLLEEN POWELL McLEAN, JD

SLACK

4/84

Copyright © 1984 by SLACK Incorporated

All rights reserved. No part of this book may be reproduced, stored in a retrieval system or transmitted in any form or by any means, electronic, mechanical, photocopying, recording or otherwise, without written permission from the publisher, except for brief quotations embodied in critical articles and reviews.

Printed in the United States of America

Library of Congress Catalog Card Number: 83-61085

ISBN: 0-943432-06-5

Published by: SLACK Incorporated
           6900 Grove Rd.
           Thorofare, NJ 08086

Last digit is print number: 8 7 6 5 4 3 2 1

To

Lois Heath and Berton John Kemp

and

Mary Earline and Kellie LeAnn Powell

Contents

Acknowledgments ix
Introduction xi
CHAPTER 1   HISTORICAL OVERVIEW 1

**CHAPTER 2   BASIC ISSUES RELATED TO
PROVISION OF MENTAL HEALTH SERVICES** 7
   Confidentiality and Privilege 7
   Release of Information 8
   Access to Records 9
   Duty to Warn Third Parties 9
   Informed Consent 12
   Competency of the Individual 15
      Guardianship 15
   Power of Attorney 17
   Distinction between Outpatient and Inpatient Care 17

**CHAPTER 3   ADMISSIONS TO PSYCHIATRIC
FACILITIES** 21
   Least Restrictive Alternative 21
   Types of Admissions 22
      Voluntary Admission 22
      Emergency Commitment 24
      Indefinite Commitment (Civil Commitment) 25
   Mandatory Outpatient Treatment 28

**CHAPTER 4   THE RIGHTS OF PATIENTS IN
INSTITUTIONS** 31
   Civil Rights of Patients 31
   Access to Patient Records 32
   Review of Patient Records 32
   Least Restrictive Alternative 33
   Seclusion and Restraints 33
   Inpatient Work 34
   Payment for Hospitalization 35
   Right to Treatment 35
   Behavioral Modification 38
   Research on the Mentally Ill 39
   Right to Aftercare 40
   Advocacy 41

CHAPTER 5   THE RIGHT TO REFUSE TREATMENT 45
  Rennie v. Klein 45
  Rogers v. Okin 49
  Current Conclusions 50
  Recent Developments 52
  Current State of the Law 54
  Electroconvulsive Therapy 56
  Psychosurgery 57

CHAPTER 6   FORENSIC ISSUES 61
  Introduction 61
  Forensic Evaluations 62
    General Guidelines 62
    Competency to Stand Trial 62
    Criminal Responsibility (Insanity Defense) 64
  Mental Health Services to Persons
    Convicted of Crimes 65
  "Criminal" Commitments 67
    Treatment of Forensic Patients 67
    Incompetent Defendants 67
    Persons Found Not Guilty by Reason of Insanity 68
    Persons Convicted of Crimes 69
  Emerging Issues 70
  Conclusion 73

CHAPTER 7   THE RIGHTS OF CHILDREN 77

CHAPTER 8   MALPRACTICE ISSUES 81
  Elements of Negligence 81
  Case Examples 82
    Abille v. United States of America 82
    Ray v. Ameri-Care Hospital 84
    Delicata v. Bourlesses 84
  Documentation 86
  The Nurse as a Witness 87
  Vicarious Liability 88
  Other Standards of Care 89

CONCLUSION 91

INDEX 93

Acknowledgments

The authors would like to express their special thanks to Ellen Pryor, Marthagem Whitlock, Alexander Brooks, Erline Gore and Lois H. Kemp for many hours spent in reviewing and commenting on the manuscript.

Continual encouragement, for which we are grateful, was offered by our colleagues Sara K. Archer, Judy Jean Chapman, Barbara Grimes, Tivis Nelson, Sallie Wamsley, Myrth York, and Susan and Joel Moseley. Robert J. Laben should be commended for his patience over many months.

Special thanks to Phronietta Kendrick and Linda Haley who typed a readable manuscript based on frequently illegible handwriting and poorly typed copy.

Lastly, we would like to acknowledge our debt to those forensic patients who were detained for years without adequate health care and judicial intervention. It was their plight that piqued our interest in communicating to mental health professionals, especially nurses, about the recent changes in mental health law.

```
        MEDICAL LIBRARY
ST. JOSEPH MERCY HOSPITAL
      660 CLINTON STREET
      DETROIT, MI 48226
```

Introduction

Both authors have had extensive experience in working in state institutions as well as with community agencies. In these roles, Ms. Laben as a psychiatric nurse and a lawyer, and Ms. MacLean as an administrator and a lawyer, have observed the frustration and problems precipitated by the increased demands on mental health professionals to understand and respond to legal issues. This is particularly true for professionals who have received extensive education in their clinical specialties but little support or training in regard to the accompanying legal issues.

During the past twenty years the intervention of the legal system in mental health issues and subsequent litigation have resulted in more change in mental health facilities and programs than in the prior two hundred years of our country's existence. Although these changes have been occasionally disruptive and the cost of litigation substantial, most professionals recognize that the ultimate result of the increased role of the legal system in setting standards for mental health care has, indeed, been to improve conditions, expand services, and increase the number and type of mental health professionals who provide these services. Therefore, it is well worth the time of all mental health professionals to become knowledgeable about mental health-legal issues, not only for the purpose of protecting themselves but also to protect the rights of patients and improve care through "preventive thinking."

After reviewing the massive number of cases and articles relating to mental health-legal issues, we concluded that it is an almost impossible task to comprehensively summarize the issues outlined in these materials. Therefore, it is not our objective to be a "catalogue" of citations for cases and articles, but to provide an outline of the basic concepts so that the professional can successfully identify pertinent legal issues. Our goal is also for this book to be useful as a resource for psychiatric-mental health nurses; however, *we are in no way attempting to provide a substitute for legal advice or a knowledge of specific state statutory and case law.* After identifying a legal issue, the professional should not only utilize his or her own knowledge of the applicable state and federal law *but also seek legal advice.*

An additional objective is to point out and acknowledge the contradiction and misapplication of certain legal trends. For professionals who have recently entered the mental health field, these contradictions must be particularly confusing. One example is the theory espoused by Thomas Szasz, a well-known psychiatrist and author, who advocates the total abolition of involuntary commitment in order to prevent the intrusion of government into the lives of the mentally ill. However, no one has ever fully reviewed the possibility that the consequences of this action would be to force society to treat the mentally ill who refuse treatment as "criminals" when their behavior is dangerous because no option of commitment exists. We must at least acknowledge that society will not tolerate certain behavior and will demand that some action be taken to isolate such individuals; and if the option of "civil" commitment is abolished, the inevitable result will be the "criminalization" of the mentally ill who exhibit dangerous behavior.

Another illustration of conflicting legal concepts is the right to refuse treatment versus the right to treatment in the least restrictive environment. Since the introduction of pharmacotherapy, more individuals have been able to function in the community rather than remain for long periods in an institution. Recent cases which recognize the right of an involuntarily committed patient to refuse treatment, including medication, may result in the increased use of inpatient facilities because of the patient's refusal to take medication and the subsequent exacerbation of the illness.

A discussion of the importance of adequate recording and reporting will be included in this monograph. Written communication of treatment has been an important aspect of health care for a long period of time, but the practice of peer audit of nursing care to evaluate professional performance is a relatively recent innovation. Because of increased litigation concerning care of the mentally disabled and the requirement of audits by accrediting organizations, mental health care givers must realize that services provided to clients will be evaluated not only by an employing organization but potentially by outside organizations such as governmental agencies and the judicial system.

Legal issues related to care of the mentally retarded will not be specifically discussed in this monograph although many legal problems that concern this group also impact on the mentally ill. These include such issues as rights in institutions, guardianship and zoning for community group homes.

Although the content of this book is directed toward psychiatric nurses, other mental health professionals will find it useful since they will be faced with the same legal issues in clinical practice with clients in institutions and the community.

CHAPTER 1
Historical Overview

Only in the past one hundred years have laws governing the commitment and treatment of the mentally ill been enacted. By looking at the historical treatment of the mentally ill, the dramatic impact of recent litigation can be placed in proper perspective.

Commitment to mental institutions was not practiced until the first part of the last century,[1] but the isolation of mentally and physically defective children on mountainsides and in pits is documented as early as 800 B.C. in Sparta.[2]

After the 1400s beliefs in witchcraft became prevalent in Europe, and the colonists who came to America brought their beliefs with them. Accusations, convictions and punishment for witchcraft did occur.[3] The practice of medicine had not evolved sufficiently to identify mental illness, its cause, or proper treatment.

During the reign of King Edward II of England, between 1255 and 1290, the *De Praerogative Regis* was passed. This law established, for the first time, two "classes" of mentally disordered individuals—the idiots and the lunatics. The term "idiot" was used to refer to persons born without understanding, and "lunatics," according to the law, were born with understanding, but lost it later in life.[4]

The law gave the feudal overlord "...the right to seize the lands of idiots in payment of the military service owed him by the mentally defective vassals."[5] Lunatics, on the other hand, might at some time recover from their illness and be able to perform their duties for the overlord; and for this reason, their lands could not be seized. A guardian, the king, was appointed through the Court of Chancery, and had the power and prerogative to use the proceeds of the lunatics' properties for their support.[6]

Founded in 1247, Saint Mary of Bethlehem in England was one of the first hospitals to provide for care of the mentally ill. It admitted "lunatics" beginning in the fifteenth century. Nicknamed "Bedlam," the hospital is reported to have used chains and irons in its "treatment" of the mentally ill inmates.[7]

In colonial America the family cared for its mentally ill members, and local tax money was available if a family was not able to adequately provide for the support of its mentally ill member.[8] If the mentally ill person was indigent and without family care or support, it was not uncommon for the individual to join a band of indigents, who together would roam the country, living off the land. In America prior to the mid-eighteenth century, many mentally ill individuals were "confined in local almshouses and jails and treated as common criminals and paupers."[9]

America's first institution to care for the mentally ill was the Pennsylvania Hospital in Philadelphia, established in 1752. In 1773 the first public mental hospital was opened at Williamsburg, Virginia, with a "keeper," rather than a doctor, in control of the institution.[10]

Benjamin Rush, considered the father of psychiatry in this country, in 1812 wrote the first publication about mental illness in America, discussing the moral treatment begun by Philippe Pinel of France and William Tuke of England. The followers of the moral treatment theory advocated treating the mentally ill with kindness and humanitarianism. Although he briefly discussed moral treatment, the major portion of Rush's treatise discussed blood-letting and "the use of the lash and of the chain and of the propriety of putting the patient in fear of death if the depleting methods already mentioned should not be effective."[11]

During the second quarter of the nineteenth century, there was a large immigration of ethnic minorities and a substantial increase in urban growth in this country. These factors, coupled with economic depression and unemployment, led to increased numbers of mentally ill. The condition induced the Secretary of State of New York to author a report which "fostered an increase in institutional care for dependent groups, with the care and treatment of the insane linked with welfare and dependence measures."[12]

In 1841 Dorothea Dix, while conducting a class for female convicts in West Cambridge jail in Massachusetts, discovered insane inmates living in the prison. This discovery led her to examine almshouses, jails, and hospitals for the mentally ill. She found conditions in these institutions so deplorable that she devoted a considerable amount of time to traveling across the nation encouraging state legislatures to build hospitals to house and care for the mentally ill.

Throughout her travels, Dix advocated moral and humanitarian treatment of the mentally ill and the construction of institutions to house them. Despite her considerable efforts, however, the mentally ill frequently were sent to asylums without planning, and the moral treatment she favored was not effectively continued.[13] Although she did make some progress, many of the hospitals were located in isolated, rural areas, thus breaking the patients' ties with their families, which is now recognized as detrimental to the treatment of the mentally ill.

Care and treatment reached a turning point in America in the 1860s owing to the experience of an Illinois woman, Mrs. E. P. W. Packard. Reportedly sane, Mrs. Packard was committed to the Illinois State Hospital by her husband. This act was permitted under an 1851 state commitment law that allowed a man to commit his wife to an institution, virtually without cause.

Mrs. Packard published several reports of her treatment in the hospital. Upon her release she devoted a considerable amount of time and money in an effort to alter the law. Not unlike Dorothea Dix, Mrs. Packard traveled extensively for several years, addressing state legislatures and campaigning to change state commitment laws. In several states she was successful. In those jurisdictions, laws were altered to provide such procedural safeguards as notice of commitment and trial by jury to determine insanity.[14]

During the 1870s, many states passed legislation that included safeguards preventing commitment of sane individuals. The guidelines for the legislation were patterned after the safeguards inherent in criminal law. In somes states, a jury was impaneled to decide the mental status of individuals. In spite of the apparent progressiveness of these laws, those judged mentally ill were committed for indefinite periods, and upon commitment they relinquished all civil rights.[15]

In 1890 New York passed the State Care Act, which divided the state into districts, each with a state hospital responsible for caring for the district's mentally ill patients. Supervision of the care of these individuals was coordinated by the State Commission on Lunacy, a name later changed to the State Department of Mental Hygiene.[16] The name change was significant because it reflected a modification in attitudes toward treatment of the mentally ill. By the end of the nineteenth century, many hospitals for the mentally ill had been constructed, and the care and treatment were primarily under the control of the state system.[17] The work of the pioneers in the field had demonstrated the need for an organized, sanctioned method of dealing with the problem of growing numbers of mentally ill people, and state hospital systems were the result. Care of the mentally ill remained materially unchanged until the latter part of this century. The mental health system, under the direction of state governments, functioned within rigid confines until after World War II.

As expertise in the psychiatric field developed, psychiatrists maintained that laws modeled after criminal law were not satisfactory. Psychiatrists throughout the United States began to criticize commitment laws which overlooked advances that had been made in psychiatry and began advocating less formal judicial proceedings which favored admissions based on medical and psychiatric opinion. It was their position that the inclusion of psychiatrists in the admissions process reduced the likelihood that wrongful commitments could take place, and that protection procedures were no longer necessary.

In 1952 the National Institute of Mental Health published a document entitled the Draft Act Governing Hospitalization of the Mentally Ill. The publication, in an effort to ease and broaden patients' access to hospitals and the treatment they provided, advocated voluntary admissions based on certifications by physicians, as well as more formal procedures when indefinite commitment was necessary. The Draft Act Governing Hospitalization not only placed emphasis on primary treatment of the mentally ill, but it also sought virtually to remove judicial intervention from the admission process by advocating notice of hearing and jury trial *after* admission rather than before.

Largely as a result of the criticism of psychiatrists and the actions of the National Institute of Mental Health, many states adopted the procedures advocated. Medical, rather than judicial, certification became prevalent. As the movement grew, so too did the potential for abuse of due process procedures for mentally ill individuals.

In the 1960s the New York Bar Association conducted a study which concluded that only ten percent of the patients committed to psychiatric institutions in New York actually had a hearing, and that patients usually did not receive notice of the hearing.[18] In 1961 the Joint Commission on Mental Illness and Health published a report stating that the institutional system of mental health care in this country had been a dismal failure.[19] The report led to the passage of the Community Mental Health Centers Act of 1963, which authorized monies for the construction of comprehensive centers to be completed over a period of years. As the comprehensive centers were built, the populations in state mental hospitals did decrease. Despite lower hospital populations, however, not everyone was satisfied with hospital treatment of the mentally ill.

Just as the pendulum had swung in favor of the intervention of physicians in the early sixties, the movement was reversed in the early seventies when activist lawyers began filing cases based on patients' rights and, specifically, the right to treatment while hospitalized. The explosion of suits filed to improve mental health care continues, and there has been a growing trend toward suits based on the patient's right to refuse treatment.

Many of the abuses in state hospitals have been alleviated through the discharge of large numbers of patients, increased funding to improve quality of care available in state hospitals, and the employment of professional instead of lay personnel. With the discharge of patients from mental hospitals, yet another problem has arisen. In the past few years, large numbers of ex-patients have been dismissed from the protective environment offered by hospitals and institutions and are wandering the streets without adequate aftercare.

In recent years, ongoing care and treatment in inpatient and community settings have become relatively common and successful. Current cutbacks in funding for these projects have somewhat diminished their effectiveness simply because there are inadequate funds to treat the large numbers of people who need this type of supervised care. However, because the facilities still operate, there is still a continuing potential for this less restrictive treatment.

Trends in the mental health field have changed dramatically in the past hundred years. The problems of treating the mentally ill have created their own concerned experts, including mental health and legal professionals. They each have their own particular concern for the plight of the mentally ill, and each has contributed to advances in the field.

Although nurses have been employed in mental health facilities for years, only recently have nurses with specialized education been utilizing this knowledge to make an impact on mental health care. With the formation of specialty groups in psychiatric nursing and the nurse-lawyer association, it is anticipated that nurses, as a group, will voice their concerns about mental health care with increasing frequency.

Since mental health laws vary widely from state to state, it is important for nurses in each state to maintain lines of communication and support in advocating the rights of patients.

REFERENCES

1. Richard B. Saphire: The Civilly Committed Public Mental Patient and the Right to Aftercare. Florida State University Law Review 4:232, 1975, p. 238.
2. Marcia P. Burgdorf and Robert Burgdorf Jr.: A History of Unequal Treatment: The Qualifications of Handicapped Persons as a 'Suspect Class' Under the Equal Protection Clause. Santa Clara Lawyer 18:855, 1975, p. 883.
3. John Biggs Jr.: The Guilty Mind. New York, Harcourt, Brace and Co., 1955, p. 62.
4. S. Sheldon Glueck: Mental Disorder and the Criminal Law. Boston, Kraus Reprint Corp., 1925, p. 128. Also, Holly Wilson and Carol R. Kneisl: Forensic Considerations in Psychiatric Nursing. In Psychiatric Nursing, Menlo Park, CA, Addison-Wesley Publishing Co., 1979, p. 723.
5. Glueck: Mental Disorder, p. 125.
6. Ibid., p. 126
7. Wilson and Kneisl: Forensic Considerations, p. 723.
8. Saphire: The Civilly Committed Patient, p. 239.
9. Ibid.
10. Richard Allen Zenoff, Elyce Ferster, and Jesse Rubin: Readings in Law and Psychiatry, rev. ed. Baltimore, The Johns Hopkins University Press, 1975, pp. 6, 7.
11. Ibid. p. 6.
12. Wilson and Kneisl: Forensic Considerations, p. 726.
13. Ibid.
14. Ibid., p. 728.
15. Ibid.
16. Ibid., p. 729.
17. Norman Dain: The Chronic Mental Patient in Nineteenth Century America. Psychiatric Annals 10:9, September 1980, p. 19.
18. Wilson and Kneisl: Forensic Considerations, p. 730.
19. Ibid, p. 729.

CHAPTER 2
Basic Issues Related to Provision of Mental Health Services

Confidentiality and Privilege

Understanding the issues of confidentiality and privilege is imperative when providing therapeutic care for patients or clients. (For the purpose of this book, the term "patient" is used for the inpatient setting; "client" is used for individuals treated in the community.) Confidentiality is the legal and ethical responsibility to keep all information concerning patients and clients private; therefore, nurses as well as other health professionals must not divulge or release information given or available to them as part of their professional duties.

Privilege is a narrower concept than confidentiality. It is created by statute to protect information elicited from clients and is granted only to specified professionals to insure that the information will be kept private and confidential. Specifically, privilege means that the stated professional can not release any information received from the client. Such privilege has been traditionally granted through statutes to lawyers, ministers, priests, and physicians. With the expansion of mental health services, other professionals such as psychologists have been added in some states.

Privilege can only be asserted by the client and does not exist unless some kind of professional, therapeutic relationship exists.[1] Privilege pertains only to information obtained during the therapeutic relationship without third party witnesses. The patient or client has the right to waive the privilege and ask for information to be given to a requesting source. The privilege is the client's and not the professional's. One state, however, has allowed an exception to the waiver just discussed. Illinois allows a psychiatrist the right to refuse a waiver in the interest of a patient.[2]

Confidentiality is a broad concept governed by state statutes and professional ethical codes which prohibits all professionals involved in the provision of mental health care to release information about specific clients unless requested by the clients or otherwise permitted by law. Almost every state has a specific statute governing confidentiality and the manner in which that information is released. This is a statute with which all nurses should be familiar.

In recent years, there has been a loss of control by patients and clients over the dissemination of private health information to insurance companies, health care facilities, employers, and the government.[3] In addition, secretaries, billing clerks, and other personnel may have access to an individual's record. All staff who have access to this information should be trained to avoid unnecessary revelations concerning a client's health care status. Health professionals have been observed discussing patient care on elevators, in halls, and in radiology departments in close proximity to other patients and visitors.

When working with patients and clients in a psychiatric setting, it is important to be aware that a patient may not want anyone to know that mental health care is being provided. Secrecy is a primary concern of many patients. Slovenko points out that "treatment of mental disorders is more clandestine than treatment of physical disorders."[4] If one calls a general hospital to inquire about a patient, the operator is free to acknowledge that the person is hospitalized. However, this generally is not true when inquiries are made about a patient in a psychiatric hospital. Acknowledgment of the person's presence in the facility is usually prohibited by the state statutory provisions regarding confidentiality.

Release of Information

Before information is released to another agency, ordinarily it is imperative that proper authorization be provided. Professionals should never release information based on a telephone inquiry unless they can determine that the person has a right to the information and can confirm the identity of the inquirer. The most common method of authorization is a release form signed by the client. The form should include certain information, such as precisely what information can be released, to whom, and for what period of time.[5] Additionally, most state confidentiality statutes authorize the release of information pursuant to a court order even if the client objects. If the state statute authorizes release only by a court order, a subpoena (which can be issued unilaterally by an attorney) does not provide proper legal authority for release. However, it is imperative that the professional respond to the subpoena by requesting that it be quashed or that a court order be issued.

Dissemination of information that may be legally released under the confidentiality statute may be prohibited if obtained through a privileged relationship. If the client does not authorize release of privileged information, the professional may have to refuse to provide such data, even if a court order is issued. This dilemma would require the professional to go through a court hearing to resolve the question.

Halleck specifies a situation in which a professional would be obligated to report confidential information without the regularly required release or court order. One example is an airline pilot who is abusing alcohol or drugs. Such a fact would have to be reported to the physician for the agency involved, based on the doctrine of obligation to the welfare of others.[6] Another exception is when the client's acts may threaten a third party. This exception is discussed later in this chapter.

Access to Records

Courts have generally assumed that the medical record of the hospital or clinic belongs to the institution or health care facility, and that the information belongs to the patient or client.[7] Some states have laws mandating a person's access to his own records, but even in those states it may be difficult for the person to obtain the record unless it is released to a physician or an attorney.[8] Halleck comments that there is a good case for allowing nonpsychiatric patients to have right of access to their records. He has some reservations about allowing a psychiatric patient to examine his own record, especially if he is acutely disturbed. According to Dr. Halleck, the patient could misinterpret the data or could be frightened by the contents.[9]

Stein and associates studied the effects of patient access to records on staff and patients in a psychiatric unit of a community general hospital. Patients reported they felt better informed, and the staff said that they contemplated more extensively what they wrote in the records. Staff availability to discuss the contents of the records seemed important to the success of the program.[10]

Duty to Warn Third Parties

An additional exception to confidentiality and privilege has developed as a result of a landmark decision in California, *Tarasoff v. Regents of the University of California.*[11] A young man, Prosenjit

Poddar, was treated by a psychologist at the University of California. He communicated to the therapist his intention of killing a young woman who was out of the country at the time of the threat. The psychologist called campus security, who stopped Mr. Poddar but determined that he did not need to be detained. There were no further therapeutic interventions by the psychologist.

When the young woman, Tatiana Tarasoff, returned to California, she was killed by the young man. Her family brought suit against the University of California. The Supreme Court of California ruled that when a therapist determines that an individual presents a danger to another individual, there is a duty to warn the intended victim. In this particular instance, the confidential relationship must cease, because "the protection of privileges ends where the public peril begins."[12]

More recently, there have been two other decisions that have reviewed the issues presented by the ruling of Tarasoff. In *McIntosh v. Milano*, a New Jersey case, Dr. Milano was treating an adolescent boy who had been involved with drugs. He had fantasies about a young woman who lived next door and expressed some jealousy toward her, which he communicated to the therapist. He carried a knife and showed the weapon to Dr. Milano. The young woman was later murdered by the adolescent, and a wrongful death action was brought by the deceased's mother against the psychiatrist for his failure to warn the intended victim. The court noted that while confidentiality is important, it is not the only consideration. The welfare of the individual and the community must come first, particularly if the duty to disclose is compelled by law or if an imminent danger to the patient or society exists.[13]

In a Nebraska decision, *Lipari v. Sears and Roebuck*, the Tarasoff concept was adopted. Ulysses L. Criff had been hospitalized at a Veterans Administration Hospital for psychiatric care. While participating in a Day Care Program, he purchased a gun. He later withdrew from the program, against medical advice. Approximately six weeks later, he entered a restaurant and fired shots into a crowded dining room, killing Dennis Lipari and seriously wounding his wife. The estate of the deceased brought suit against the store and the government. The negligence law of the state of Nebraska was applied.

> To summarize, this Court is of the opinion that under Nebraska law the relationship between a psychotherapist and his patient gives rise to an affirmative duty for the benefit of third persons. This duty requires that the therapist initiate whatever precau-

tions are reasonably necessary to protect potential victims of this patient. This duty arises only when in accordance with the standards of his profession, the therapist knows or should know that his patient's dangerous propensities present an unreasonable risk of harm to others.[14]

In this particular instance, as well as in most others of this nature, involuntary commitment of the individual to a mental health facility would have been the most effective procedure to protect the victim. The therapist must take the same actions as other reasonably prudent professionals would in the same circumstances.[15]

In California a decision was rendered by the Supreme Court that has been labeled shocking.[16] A young man, James, was released from an institution to the custody of his mother. James had indicated that if released, he would kill an unidentified child in his neighborhood. Within 24 hours of James' release, he assaulted and murdered the plaintiff's son, who was five years of age. The victim's parents brought a law suit for wrongful death.

The Court ruled that because there was no specific identifiable victim, no duty existed to protect the youngster. The Court also relied on a public policy consideration which would allow public officials to release prisoners, residents, and patients without assuming risk of liability for mistakes.[17]

In Maryland, a lawsuit was brought against a psychiatric team—a psychiatrist (deceased), a psychiatric nurse, and a psychologist. A couple experiencing marital problems was in group therapy. The wife had an affair with another member of the group, a dentist; and the husband, finding the wife in bed with him, shot the dentist but did not kill him.

A suit was brought against the team, who knew of the liaison, for failure to warn the dentist of the potential danger. The judge ruled in favor of the defendants on the basis of the confidentiality of the psychiatrist, psychologist-patient relationship. "The lips of the psychiatrist or psychologist have been statutorily sealed shut subject to being unsealed by the patient or the patient's authorized representative."[18]

A survey study published in the *Stanford Law Review* indicates that psychiatrists and psychologists who responded to a questionnaire were aware of the Tarasoff decision. It was concluded that a potential victim was more likely to be warned by therapists post-Tarasoff than prior to the decision. It was also noted that there was an increased likelihood of consultation with others, and that record keeping had been changed. Some therapists stopped keeping detailed records, while others began keeping more detailed records. The latter was done to justify decisions that had been implemented.[19]

Many therapists have been appalled at the implications of the Tarasoff decision and feel it greatly impinges on the therapist-patient relationship. Wexler suggests that there might be some interesting therapeutic interventions as a result of the Tarasoff decision. If the potential victim is a family member, that individual might be brought into the therapeutic situation, and a shift from the intrapsychic to an interactions model might be developed. "Perhaps more precisely, Tarasoff may lead mental health professionals to practice the paradigm currently resisted but already accepted and preached by the bulk of the scientific and clinical literature."[20]

Nursing Implications. It is important to maintain confidential relationships with patients and clients. Nurses should establish whether or not the statutory privilege has been enacted by legislatures in their states and whether or not it includes nursing privilege. If a nurse does not have privileged communication, she should be especially alert for situations in which she might be compelled to testify or become subject to a penalty of contempt of court if she refuses.

The duty to warn victims has been established in several states, and the nurse should be cognizant of this fact when working in a psychotherapeutic relationship with a patient. Kjervik believes that the principles of the Tarasoff decision could be extended to involve a psychiatric nurse therapist.[21]

Informed Consent

The right of an individual to be adequately informed about a procedure or treatment to be implemented by a health professional has long been established. The recent consumer movement, along with the growing trend toward mental health clients questioning prescribed treatments, will focus even more attention on the issue of informed consent.

It is a basic premise that competent adults have the right to decide what they will authorize to be done to their own bodies.[22] Case law and recently published literature set out the following important components of informed consent: (1) An individual must be mentally competent and understand the procedures to which he is consenting.[23] (2) The individual must have enough information on which to base a decision, including material risks. A risk is considered material when a reasonable person would "attach significance to the risk or cluster of risks in deciding whether or not to forgo the proposed therapy."[24] (3) There should also be a description of the available alternatives to the proposed treatment and the "dangers inherently and potentially involved in each."[25] (4) It should be noted that consent can be withdrawn at any time.[26] According to VanBiervliet, the more intrusive the procedure, the greater the need for informed consent.[27]

There are two exceptions to the requirement of informed consent and subsequent disclosure. The first exception applies to an unconscious patient whose condition would worsen without a particular procedure, when the benefit outweighs the potential harm of the proposed treatment plan.[28] The second exception is one that has been delegated to the physician to protect an individual who would suffer severe detriment to his well-being as a result of disclosure.[29] With the recent mental health consumer movement, this second exception should be carefully assessed.

One of the major problems in obtaining informed consent from a mental health client is the ability of the individual to comprehend the information that is given to him. Unless an individual has been found incompetent to manage his affairs, he is considered able to make decisions for himself. It is difficult, however, to maintain that a psychotic voluntary patient always has the understanding necessary to consent to treatment procedures. Ashley points out that several authors have drawn attention to "lack of comprehension on the part of a sample of mental patients as to the terms of their voluntary status."[30] However, this was not limited to mental patients but included medical patients who knew less than the mental patients about their medication.[31] In a recent study conducted at a state mental hospital in Massachusetts, only 8.4% of 261 patients in a study group could give the name of at least one of their prescribed medications, including its frequency of administration and desired effect.[32] The Olins found that 8% of residents at a state hospital could articulate the terms of their voluntary admission.[33] Based on these studies, it is clear that health professionals will have to be diligent in providing information to clients so that the clients will be knowledgeable enough to give consent. After consent is obtained, health care personnel should be attuned to reinforcing provided information.

Annas points out that there is some authority for a spouse to authorize consent for an incompetent patient.[34] In one case, the court ruled that a father could consent to treatment of an adult son with electroconvulsive therapy (ECT).[35] Annas concludes that in light of the recent rights movement for mental patients, it is prudent to have a legal guardian appointed, especially if the procedure is elective. He also suggests that it is the custom in the medical community to request consent of the next of kin. Although consent may not be binding, it may waive the rights of the relative "to any future legal action."[36] In obtaining consent from an incompetent patient, legal advice should be sought if there is any question.

Solomon suggests that in situations that involve involuntary patients, detailed written agreements or oral tape-recorded agreements should be made part of the permanent records. These would serve as contracts between patients and therapists and would be reviewed and renegotiated if necessary. In addition, it is suggested that these agreements be reviewed by an independent third party. The author points out that the feasibility of this kind of arrangement is dependent upon the patient's condition, level of literacy, and willingness to participate.[37]

Traditionally, doctors have obtained informed consent for the procedures that they were to perform. Sometimes this responsibility is delegated to the nurse. If the nurse determines that the patient does not adequately understand the procedure the physician is to perform, the nurse should notify the physician or appropriate administrator.[38] Mancini emphasizes that if the procedure is to be performed by the nurse, consent should be obtained by the nurse.[39]

Zerubavel points out a very interesting phenomenon that occurs during the admission of a patient to a psychiatric facility. Since many mental health facilities utilize a team approach, each person on the team may assume that another individual has discussed information relating to informed consent and the rights of the patient. Zerubavel terms this "floating responsibility." He comments that physicians are personally responsible for patients, whereas nurses, because of shift changes, are not. "Nurses' responsibility of patients is almost entirely impersonal and is hardly ever expected to even transcend the temporal boundaries of their shifts."[40] Some would criticize this observation, but with the movement in many areas toward primary nursing, this criticism could be diminished.

Nursing Implications. Nurses should become acutely aware of the importance of providing information to clients about nursing procedures. If a client has questions pertaining to the procedure or to administration of medications, answers should be given as clearly and succinctly as possible. If queries arise concerning a medical procedure, the physician should be notified. It should also be noted that the client can revoke consent for a treatment or procedure at any time. The issue of right to refuse treatment is discussed later.

Competency of the Individual

GUARDIANSHIP

In most instances, an individual who is older than eighteen is permitted to manage his own property and health in any manner that he desires. Although a person may appear to be incompetent to handle his property or person, he is still legally competent until a court declares him legally incompetent and appoints a guardian or conservator to act on his behalf, either as guardian of his estate or guardian of his person, or both. All states have statutory provisions specifying when and how a person can be declared incompetent. Traditionally, the procedures have been informal and applied primarily to elderly or mentally disabled persons. There are also specific procedures for establishing guardianship of minors.

The changes that have taken place in limiting the use of mental hospitals have resulted in a renewed focus on the utilization of guardianship procedures and the definition of incompetency. Incompetency is a different issue than involuntary commitment to an inpatient psychiatric facility. In the past, persons who were involuntarily committed were also frequently declared incompetent to handle their affairs. However, in the 1960s the issues of competency and commitability were clearly separated; an individual who was involuntarily committed to a facility retained all his rights, including the right to manage his affairs. The only rights a person loses when involuntarily committed are the right to leave the facility and, until recently, the right to refuse psychiatric treatment.

Ironically, the legal assault on the use of civil commitment and the emerging right of patients to refuse treatment have resulted in greater use of guardianship procedures. Many states have revised their guardianship and conservatorship laws to provide more stringent due process protection and to provide a more specific definition of incompetency. The result of the reform has been the creation of a limited guardianship, which permits the court to declare a person incompetent only in those areas in which he cannot function, rather than declaring him totally competent or incompetent. By 1980, sixteen states had given judges the authority to limit the powers of the guardian, ten had adopted limited guardianship statutes, and eight more were considering such proposals.[41]

While there is general agreement about the need for more due process and more stringent standards in guardianship proceedings, there is extensive disagreement about the role that the guardian should play in seeking mental health care, particularly since the use of involuntary commitment has been greatly restricted. For example, Dr. Lee Haller, a psychiatrist, has stated that the appointment of a guardian of the person is the solution to providing care to seriously mentally ill persons who refuse voluntary psychiatric treatment and who do not meet the involuntary commitment standards.[42] Haller suggests that a guardian will usually have the legal authority to "volunteer" the ward for treatment.

In fact, state laws vary regarding whether a guardian is specifically permitted or denied the power to commit his ward to a psychiatric facility if judicial commitment proceedings have not been initiated. Since the United States Supreme Court has not reviewed this issue, guardians in states where the statutes do not specify this exclusion are generally permitted to "voluntarily" admit their wards for psychiatric treatment. Some professionals, particularly lawyers, maintain that this procedure is an improper use of guardianship statutes because it is used to circumvent judicial commitment statutes.[43]

It has also been pointed out that the wording of some limited guardianship statutes has in fact expanded the use of limited guardianship to include individuals who previously would not have been declared incompetent.[44] Other lawyers have asserted that the use of guardianship is so arbitrary and abused that alternatives should be found.[45] However, it is unlikely that the use of guardianship will diminish unless the United States Supreme Court rules on the issue. Until then, it is important to check the law of the state where you are practicing.

Nursing Implications. The important point that a mental health professional should remember is that a client is competent unless a court has declared him incompetent. Before beginning the treatment of any client, it is good practice to clarify whether or not a guardian has been appointed. If so, a copy of the court order should be obtained so that the limits of the guardian's authority will be clear. On the other hand, if a clearly incompetent client has not been declared legally incompetent, this information should be communicated to the administration of the facility and the family.

Power of Attorney

The power of attorney is occasionally suggested as a method of handling the affairs of an individual who is incompetent. A power of attorney is a written instrument authorizing one individual to act as another's agent or attorney, in either a specific or an unlimited manner. The power of attorney chiefly has been used to facilitate the conducting of business when the primary person cannot be physically present. It is also used for an elderly person or one with physical limitations.

However, the power of attorney has limited usefulness for persons who are actually incompetent, and it should not be used as a method to circumvent the guardianship laws. If a competent person executes a power of attorney and later becomes incompetent, it is a matter of state law whether the power of attorney remains in effect. In such cases, some states permit the power of attorney to remain effective if specifically stated in the instrument.[46]

Nursing Implications. It is important to remember that the power of attorney can be used only to authorize one person to manage the estate or business affairs of another. This instrument should not be used to permit an individual to make personal or health decisions for another. Therefore, a power of attorney cannot be accepted to authorize treatment.

Distinction between Outpatient and Inpatient Care

The major distinction between outpatient and inpatient mental health care is that of voluntariness. In most states, outpatient mental health care is still provided on a voluntary basis only, as with any other health care. However, inpatient mental health care can be provided on both a voluntary and an involuntary basis. Therefore, when providing outpatient mental health care, the issues of informed consent and determining whether a person has been declared incompetent are very important. Some states have passed legislation permitting mandatory outpatient treatment under limited circumstances; the appropriate state law should be reviewed to assess whether such legislation exists.

The determination of "dangerousness" is an additional issue that has gained significance since the revised standards and procedures for involuntary commitment statutes have changed the ranges of clients currently served at the community level. Since fewer persons are hospitalized, and those who are hospitalized are detained for shorter periods, more potentially dangerous and chronic clients must be served on an outpatient basis. If a person appears to require inpatient care, the appropriate treatment should be discussed with the client so that he can make an informed decision, if possible. However, if the individual is unwilling to seek inpatient care or is posing immediate threat of harm to himself or others, a decision must be reached concerning involuntary commitment to a psychiatric facility. Also, if a person poses a threat to a third party, a decision must be made whether or not to warn this party, as discussed previously in this chapter.

REFERENCES

1. Ralph Slovenko: Accountability and Abuse of Confidentiality in the Practice of Psychiatry, International Journal of Law and Psychiatry, vol. 2, no. 4, 1979, pp. 431-454.
2. Ibid., p. 447, ftn. 53.
3. Betty Holcomb: Varied State Laws Complicate Patient Record Privacy Issue. Health Care Week, January 1, 1979, p. 8. Also, When You Apply for Insurance is Your Life an Open Book? U.S. News and World Report, May 31, 1976, p. 33. Also, William Hines: Medical Data Ethic Problems Eyed. Chicago Sun-Times, Tuesday, December 12, 1978, p. 24.
4. Slovenko: Accountability and Abuse, p. 443.
5. American Medical Record Association: Confidentiality of Patient Health Information. Chicago, Illinois, 1977.
6. Seymour Halleck: Law in the Practice of Psychiatry: A Handbook for Clinicians. New York, Plenum Publishing Corp., 1980, p. 181.
7. Mary Cazalas: Nursing and the Law, 3d. ed. Germantown, MD, Aspen Systems Corp., 1978, p. 54.
8. Alan Westin: Medical Records: Should Patients Have Access? The Hastings Center Report, December 1977, pp. 23-28.
9. Halleck: Handbook for Clinicians, p. 181.
10. Eugene Stein, et al: Patient Access to Medical Records on a Psychiatric Inpatient Unit, American Journal of Psychiatry, 136:3, March 1979, pp. 327-329.
11. *Tarasoff v. Regents of the University of California*, 592 P2d 553 (1974).
12. Ibid.
13. *McIntosh v. Milano*, 403 F2d 500 (N.J. Super. Ct. 1979). Also, Paul S. Applebaum: Tarasoff: An Update on the Duty to Warn. Hospital and Community Psychiatry, vol. 32, no. 1, January 1981, pp. 14-15. Also, Arthur Bernstein: Some Legal Consequences of Treating Mental Patients. Hospitals, February 1, 1981, p. 39.
14. *Lipari v. Sears and Roebuck*, 497 F. Supp. 185 at 193 (D.C. Neb., 1980).
15. Bernstein: Legal Consequences, p. 40.
16. Ibid.

17. *Thompson v. County of Alameda*, 614 P2d 728 (Calif. 1980).
18. *Shaw v. Glickman*, 415 A2d 625 (Maryland 1980).
19. Note, Stanford Law Review, vol. 31, November 1978, p. 165.
20. David Wexler: Patients, Therapists, and Third Parties: The Victimological Virtues of Tarasoff. International Journal of Law and Psychiatry, vol. 2, 1974, pp. 1-28, at p. 28.
21. Diane Kjervik: The Psychiatric Nurse's Duty to Warn Potential Victims of Homicidal Psychotherapy Outpatients. Law, Medicine and Health Care, vol. 9, no. 6, December 1981, pp. 11-16.
22. *Schloendorff v. Society of New York Hospital,* 211 N.W. 125, 105 N.E. 92-95 (1914).
23. Marguerite Mancini and Alice T. Gale: Emergency Care and the Law. Rockville, MD, Aspen Systems, 1981, p. 88.
24. *Canterbury v. Spence,* 464 F 2d 772, p. 787 (D.C. Cir. 1972).
25. *Cobb v. Grant,* 104 Cal. Rpt. 505, 502 P 2d 1, p. 10 (1972).
26. Mancini and Gale: Emergency Care, p. 88.
27. Alan VanBiervliet and Jan Sheldon-Wildgen: Liability Issues in Community Based Programs. Baltimore-London, Paul H. Brooks Publishing Co., 1981, p. 124.
28. *Canturbury v. Spence*, p. 788.
29. Ibid., p. 789.
30. Mary Ashley, Regina Sestak, and Loren Roth: Legislating Human Rights: Informed Consent and the Pennsylvania Mental Health Procedures Act. Bulletin of the American Academy of Psychiatry and the Law, 8 (2), pp. 133-151, at p. 134.
31. Ibid.
32. Jeffrey Geller: State Hospital Patients and Their Medication—Do They Know What They Take? American Journal of Psychiatry, 139:5, May 1982, pp. 611-615.
33. Grace Olin and Harry S. Olin: Informed Consent in Voluntary Mental Hospital Admissions. American Journal of Psychiatry, 132:9, September 1975, pp. 938-941.
34. George J. Annas and Barbara F. Glantz Katz: The Rights of Doctors, Nurses and Allied Health Professionals. Cambridge, MA, Ballinger Publishing Co., 1981, p. 79.
35. *Farver v. Olkon*, 254 P 2d 520 (Calif. 1953).
36. Annas: The Rights of Doctors, p. 80.
37. Trudy Solomon: Informed Consent for Mental Patients. Human Rights, 31, Spring 1979, pp. 31-32, 52-55.
38. Angela Holder and John Lewis: Informed Consent and the Nurse. Nursing Law and Ethics, 2 (2), pp. 1, 2, 8.
39. Mancini and Gale: Emergency Care, p. 88.
40. Eviatar Zerubavel: The Bureaucratization of Responsibility: The Case of Informed Consent. Bulletin of the American Academy of Psychiatry and the Law, vol, VIII, no. 2, pp. 161-167.
41. Report of Committee on Legal Incapacity. Limited Guardianship: Survey of Implementation Considerations. Real Property, Probate and Trust Journal, vol. 15, p. 544.

42. H. Haller: Guardianship: An Alternative to I'm Sorry. Bulletin of the American Academy of Psychiatry and the Law, vol. 7 (3), p. 296.
43. G.H. Morris: The Use of Guardianships to Achieve—or to Avoid—the Least Restrictive Alternative. International Journal of Law and Psychiatry, vol. 2, p. 99.
44. Ibid., p. 107.
45. G. Alexander: Premature Probate: A Different Perspective on Guardianship for the Elderly. Standard Law Review, vol. 31, p. 1003.
46. Tennessee Code Annotated, section 64–512.

CHAPTER 3
Admissions To Psychiatric Facilities

Least Restrictive Alternative

One of the issues confronting a mental health professional treating a mentally ill person is the alternative of referring the individual to an inpatient facility. Broadly, admissions can be classified in three categories; voluntary, emergency involuntary, and indefinite involuntary, or judicial commitment.

Each type of admission has legal implications about which mental health professionals should be aware. However, prior to any commitment, the doctrine of "least restrictive alternative" must be addressed. The concept of the "least restrictive alternative" means providing sufficient care for the client with the least restrictive methods in the least restrictive setting. The application of this idea to an inpatient setting is discussed in Chapter 4.

One of the first mental health cases to describe least restrictive alternative was *Lake v. Cameron*.[1] An elderly woman filed a writ of habeas corpus requesting her release from an institution in Washington, DC. Although it was felt by mental health care givers that she needed attention and not constant medical supervision, she was nevertheless continuously hospitalized. The court held that alternatives to confinement in a mental hospital should be investigated, including "outpatient, foster care, half-way houses, day hospitals and nursing homes."[2]

In a later case in the District of Columbia, brought as a class action suit, the court ruled that "suitable care and treatment under the least restrictive conditions are required."[3] In this particular situation, the government was mandated to develop less restrictive alternatives if such alternatives were not available. In *O'Connor v. Donaldson*, the United States Supreme Court commented that one cannot be constitutionally confined if other less restrictive alternatives are more suitable and if the person has a support system and is capable of safely surviving in the community.[4] Few statutes define the persons who shall be responsible for developing and assessing therapeutic treatment alternatives.[5] Most state commitment laws now authorize commitment only if there are no less restrictive alternatives available. However, when developing a treatment plan for an individual, *all* alternatives should be outlined, including inpatient and community treatment options. This would include analysis of the full range of alternatives, from the least to the most restrictive.

If commitment is necessary, the professionals who provide evidence at a commitment hearing should be able to list treatment alternatives in the region. Treatment options will vary depending on the location of the individual. For example, a half-way house or a day care center may not be located in a rural county, but they might be available in the neighboring area.

Types of Admissions

There are three basic types of admissions to inpatient psychiatric facilities: (1) voluntary admission, (2) emergency commitment, and (3) indefinite commitment (civil commitment).[6] State laws pertaining to these procedures apply to both public and private facilities. Of course, voluntary admission is more familiar to nurses because this is the only method of admission to general medical facilities. However, because of the nature of the illness of some psychiatric patients, the procedures related to voluntary admission must be handled with particular care.

VOLUNTARY ADMISSION

States may vary the procedures used for voluntary admission, but they all provide for the admission of persons who voluntarily request services. Usually the statute states that any person can be admitted to a psychiatric facility as a voluntary patient if he is mentally ill, in need of inpatient care, and willing to seek admission.[7] However, as a result of the increased emphasis on community treatment and the provision of services through the least restrictive alternative, a person seeking inpatient care may be referred to a community mental health center for care unless his condition or behavior requires immediate hospitalization. Additionally, the funding allotted to state hospitals has been drastically cut on the theory that it should be used to provide comprehensive community services; consequently, admissions are limited to the most serious cases. Most private institutions will accept voluntary admissions upon the referral of the treating physician.

Just as all patients must consent to admission to a general medical facility and to the subsequent treatment they receive, the psychiatric patient must also provide such consent. However, some commentators have questioned whether all psychiatric patients have the capacity to understand and to consent to such admission and treatment.[8] One state has resolved this dilemma by recognizing the informal admission, which has the same legal status as a medical admission.[9] An informal admission indicates that the patient is agreeable to admission and that no one will detain him if he insists upon leaving.

However, most nurses practice in states where only the option of a voluntary admission is available. The consent to voluntary admission and treatment consists of three elements: (1) sufficient information to enable the individual to make an informed decision, (2) the absence of coercion to ensure the voluntariness of the decision, and (3) the patient's competency to make the decision.[10] The first two elements can be addressed by designing procedures and forms to demonstrate that the person was provided with sufficient information and that he was not coerced. The problems associated with these two elements do not vary greatly between medical patients and psychiatric patients.[11] Competency, the third element of informed consent, is of particular relevance to the admission of psychiatric patients because mental illness is the most likely of all illnesses to affect competency.[12] Because voluntary entry to a psychiatric facility is the first point at which most seriously ill patients are asked to give informed consent, this procedure must be handled with care.

If a person is thought to be incompetent to consent to his own admission to a psychiatric facility, the only immediately available option is emergency commitment. However, since the condition and behavior of many mentally ill persons do not meet emergency commitment standards, this option has limited use. Another alternative is to initiate guardianship proceedings so that a guardian can consent to the admission. However, as discussed in Chapter 2, some state statutes prohibit the guardian from consenting to admission of the ward to a psychiatric facility and require that commitment proceedings be used for this purpose. Even if the guardian can legally consent to the admission, seeking guardianship is a timely and costly procedure which will not provide an immediate solution for a person who needs hospitalization.

In practice, most psychiatric facilities maintain that a person must be presumed competent if he has not been legally adjudicated incompetent by a court of law. Therefore, emphasis is placed on the procedure of informing the patient of the terms of his admission and the care he will be receiving, as well as on the procedure for documenting that the patient was not coerced. However, if there is serious question about a person's competency, and if the person meets commitment standards, the involuntary commitment process should be initiated. Otherwise most state statutes provide no viable options.

Once a person is voluntarily admitted to a psychiatric facility, he must continue to provide consent for treatment. Unlike committed patients, there is no question whether or not a voluntary patient has the right to refuse treatment. If a voluntary patient refuses treatment, the facility must find another method of treatment agreeable to the patient, release the patient, or, if the patient poses a danger to himself or others, initiate commitment proceedings.

All state statutes provide for a voluntary patient to be released within a specified period if he requests release. For example, Tennessee state law requires that such a patient be released within 8 hours of his request to leave.[13] If the staff considers the person to pose a danger to himself or others as a result of his mental illness, the director of the facility should initiate commitment proceedings.

Emergency Commitment

The second type of admission procedure is emergency commitment. When an individual is unwilling to seek treatment and poses an immediate threat of serious harm to himself or others as a result of mental illness, state statutes provide for emergency involuntary admission to a psychiatric facility. This commitment differs from indefinite judicial commitment because it permits commitment for a short period without a court hearing. Because of the potential for abuse, the standards and procedures for emergency commitment have been reviewed in a number of court decisions.[14]

Most statutes now require the threat of actual physical harm before an emergency commitment can be implemented. Usually, when a person is thought to require emergency hospitalization and refuses to seek treatment, a law enforcement official or a licensed physician is authorized by law to take the person into custody for the purpose of having him undergo a psychiatric evaluation and, if recommended by the examining physician, to provide transportation to a psychiatric facility. For example, under Tennessee law, a facility is authorized to admit a person as an emergency case if a physician or PhD psychologist certifies that the person's behavior meets the standards for emergency commitment.[15] The facility must provide a second physician also to certify that the person meets these standards. Once these two certifications have been provided, the facility may admit the person for up to five days before a probable cause hearing is held.

After the probable cause hearing, the judge must either order the patient released or held only for a specific period, for example, no more than twenty days after initial detention in Tennessee. At the end of that time, the person must be released unless a petition for indefinite commitment has been filed. It is important that the staff in the facility advise the person of the nature of his commitment and his rights under this commitment, as well as scrupulously follow the procedural requirements set out in the commitment statute.

Under most state laws, aversive therapy, such as electroconvulsive therapy, is not permitted during emergency commitment. Generally the only care permitted is the routine treatment necessary to treat the emergency condition of the patient. If at any time during the commitment the person's condition improves and he no longer meets the emergency standards, he should be released or permitted to admit himself voluntarily.

Indefinite Commitment (Civil Commitment)

The third type of admission procedure is the indefinite commitment, otherwise known as judicial commitment or civil commitment. This is the only process by which a person may be detained in a psychiatric facility against his will for an indefinite period. Most state legislators have responded to the legal attacks made on this procedure by making extensive revisions in the state commitment statutes.

The legal and historical justification for the use of indefinite commitment has been based on two theories: the *parens patriae* power of the state to take care of persons who are unable to take care of themselves, and the police power of the state to protect the public from dangerous individuals.[16] Originally, most commitment statutes relied on both theories and provided for the detention of individuals who were dangerous as well as individuals who simply required care because of their mental illness and refused to seek treatment.[17] Some court cases in the 1970s focused on the question of whether a state could constitutionally commit a person who had not exhibited dangerous behavior.[18] In other words, they speculated that only the police power and not the *parens patriae* power of the state could be relied on to justify indefinite commitment. However, other courts have justified the *parens patriae* commitment on the basis that treatment would be provided.

Chapter Three

In addition to the issues raised concerning the behavior required for commitment, the procedures used for the commitment process have also been scrutinized by the courts. Under most state statutes, this process can be initiated when an authorized official, physician, or family member files a petition for such commitment along with certification by two physicians—or mental health professionals, if provided by statute—that the individual is mentally ill, that his behavior poses a likelihood of serious harm, and that suitable community resources are unavailable. In spite of the argument that courts should limit commitments to "dangerous" persons, the standards for "likelihood of serious harm" generally are broader for indefinite commitment than for emergency commitment. The standards include immediate danger to self or others as well as more passive types of danger that can result from a person's inability to avoid or protect himself from harm because of mental illness. Some legal experts argue that because commitment results in the deprivation of liberty, the procedures used should parallel those used for civil trials. Certain authorities have gone so far as to suggest that the commitment process be abolished.[19]

Obviously, these are issues that will ultimately have to be resolved by the United States Supreme Court. The first case to be decided by the Court that involved a review of the conditions under which a mental patient may be involuntarily committed, other than in relation to criminal charges, was in 1974 in *O'Connor v. Donaldson*.[20] The specifics of *O'Connor v. Donaldson* are fully discussed in Chapter 4, "The Rights of Clients in Institutions." Although the Court was asked to review the right to treatment in this case, the Court sidestepped it. The Court did, however, state the following about the requirements for confinement: "Mere public intolerance or animosity cannot constitutionally justify the deprivation of a person's physical liberty. In short, a state cannot constitutionally confine without more a nondangerous individual who is capable of surviving safely in freedom by himself or with the help of willing and responsible family members or friends."[21] By focusing attention on certain minimal requirements for confinement, the Court delayed having to make a decision about the right to treatment. The Court neither defined the "more" required to confine the nondangerous mentally ill nor stipulated whether anything more is required to confine the dangerously mentally ill or those not capable of surviving safely in freedom with help from family and friends.[22]

Not until five years later, in 1979, did the Court again decide another civil commitment case. In *Addington v. Texas*, the Court reviewed a variety of procedural issues in indefinite commitment.[23] The major issue presented in that case was the standard of persuasion required by the Constitution. Chief Justice Burger, who authored the opinion, reached a compromise between applying the standard used in a criminal trial and the standard used in a civil trial. He reasoned that the risk of an erroneous decision in civil commitment proceedings requires the use of a standard of persuasion more rigorous than the "preponderance of the evidence" standard which is used in civil proceedings, but that the "beyond a reasonable doubt" standard required in criminal cases was unnecessary because the state sought to help, not punish.[24] Therefore he settled on the "clear and convincing" standard, a burden of proof that requires more than a "preponderance of the evidence" and less than "beyond a reasonable doubt."

The Court further held that the substantive standards for civil commitment for mental illness may vary from state to state, and that procedures must be allowed to vary as long as they meet the constitutional minimum. The opinion held that the state has legitimate interest under its *parens patriae* powers to provide care to its citizens who are unable to care for themselves because of mental illness, and that the state also has authority under its police power to protect the community from the dangerous tendencies of those who are mentally ill. Because Burger relied on the theory that the purpose of commitment laws is to help the person rather than to punish him, *Addington* leaves unclear whether or not a person who is committed only because he is dangerous should be treated any differently than a person who is committed because of his need for care. Therefore, this case does not resolve the questions left unanswered by *O'Connor*.

Justice Burger, however, expanded on his position in a concurring opinion in *Youngberg v. Romeo*, a more recent United States Supreme Court decision, a case concerning a person involuntarily committed to an institution for the mentally retarded. In this opinion, he specifically stated his belief that there is no constitutional right to "habilitation."[25] Because the concept of habilitation for a mentally retarded individual is parallel to the concept of treatment for a mentally ill person, this case is pertinent to this issue. The majority opinion held that the individual had a right to minimally adequate or reasonable training to ensure safety and freedom from undue restraint. However, the Court once again declined to rule on whether or not an individual involuntarily committed to a state institution has some general constitutional right to training per se.

Mandatory Outpatient Treatment

As a result of the limits placed on indefinite commitments by the Court, many states have experienced a problem with "revolving" patients. These are generally persons who are chronically mentally ill, improving with medication when hospitalized but regressing when released because they discontinue medication. Because these patients are repeatedly committed, one state has attempted to resolve this problem by authorizing mandatory outpatient treatment for committed patients who are likely to become dangerous in the future if they do not take medication.[26] If such persons do not follow the outpatient procedures, recommitment is simplified and expedited. However, there may be a question of increased liability for facilities that do not identify future dangerousness. Until now, facilities had only the responsibility to identify properly present behavior and dangerousness.

Nursing Implications. Whether functioning as a nurse in an outpatient or an inpatient facility, it is imperative to be acquainted with the various admission statutes in your state as well as admission procedures developed by the individual facilities. The type of admission for each patient should be clearly identified in his record because the procedures for treatment and the request to leave the facility may be handled differently depending on the admission status of the patient. Prior to the patient's admission to the facility, procedures and statutory requirements should be carefully implemented and documented. If the law is not being followed by the institution, the nurse should draw this to the attention of the administrators.

Although nurses are not generally recognized by commitment statutes as being qualified to certify the need for commitment, they might be the professionals who identify outpatient clients needing hospitalization or voluntary dangerous patients requesting to leave the facility. Commitment standards may vary in their application particularly if a person retains a knowledgeable, aggressive attorney. The outcome of commitment proceedings is not always predictable. However, nurses have the responsibility for recommending commitment proceedings for individuals whose condition, in their opinion, requires hospitalization. Therefore, it is imperative to describe behavior accurately and definitively record it in the patient's record. Mental health professionals may not always agree with the outcome of a commitment hearing; however, the patient has the right to have all information relative to his condition accurately assessed before he is involuntarily detained in an institution.

REFERENCES

1. *Lake v. Cameron,* 364 F2d 65 (D.C. Cir. 1966 en banc).
2. Ibid., pp. 659-660.
3. *Dixon v. Weinberger,* 405 F. Supp. 974 (D.C. Cir. 1975), p. 979.
4. *O'Connor v. Donaldson,* 422 U.S. 563 (1975), p. 575.
5. P. Browning Hoffman and Lawrence Foust: Least Restrictive Treatment of Mentally III: A Doctrine in Search of Its Senses. 14 San Diego Law Review 1100, p. 1119.
6. M. D. Hemelt and M. E. Mackert: Dynamics of Law in Nursing and Health Care. Reston, VA, Reston Publishing Co., 1978, pp. 101-102. Also Tennessee Code Annotated, sections 33-601, 33-603, 33-604
7. Tennessee Code Annotated, section 33-601.
8. Harold Owens: When is Voluntary Commitment Really Voluntary? American Journal of Psychiatry, 47 (1): 104-110, January 1977.
9. Ibid., p. 109.
10. M. Appelbaum, et al: Empirical Assessment of Competency to Consent to Psychiatric Hospitalization. American Journal of Psychiatry, 138:9, September 1981.
11. Ibid.
12. Ibid.
13. Tennessee Code Annotated, section 33-601.
14. *Yezerski v. Fong,* 428 A.2d 766 (Pa. Comm. Ct. 1981). Also, *Williams v. Meredith,* 407 A.2d 569 (D.C. Ct. App. 1979).
15. Tennessee Code Annotated, section 33-603.
16. R. B. Saphire: The Civilly Committed Public Mental Patient and the Right to Aftercare. Florida State University Law Review, 4:232, 1976.
17. Ibid., p. 255.
18. T. S. Szasz: Law, Liberty and Psychiatry. New York. The Macmillan Co., 1963.
19. *Lessard v. Schmidt,* 349 F. Supp. 1078 (E. D. Wis., 1974), vacated on procedural grounds 421 U.S. 957 (1975), reinstated 413 F. Supp. 1318 (E. D. Wis. 1976).
20. *O'Connor v. Donaldson,* 493 F2d 507 (Fifth Cir., 1974), vacated on other grounds 422 U.S. 563 (1975).
21. Ibid., p. 575-576.
22. Daniel Shurman: Warren Burger and the Civil Commitment Tetralogy, International Journal of Law and Psychiatry. 3:155-161 esp. p.. 156, 1980.
23. *Addington v. Texas,* 441 U.S. 418, 434 (1979).
24. Shurman: Warren Burger, p. 157.
25. *Youngberg v. Romeo,* 102 Sup. Ct. 2452 (1982).
26. Tennessee Code Annotated, section 33.

CHAPTER 4
The Rights of Patients in Institutions

When individuals are hospitalized in a mental health facility, they may be deprived of the freedom to leave the facility, but they do maintain certain legal rights. These rights are usually defined by state law, and nurses should determine whether the law in the state in which they practice specifies these rights. Of course, unless the patient is notified of the rights, they will not be effective. According to the *Mental Disability Law Reporter,* more than one-third of the states do make some provision to assure that notice of rights is given to the patients. Frequently a document is posted for reading in a location that is easily accessible to patients.[1] In some hospitals, the patient is given a listing of his rights on admission.

Civil Rights of Patients

Regardless of the differences in state law, it is particularly important to remember that unless a person has been declared incompetent prior to or at the time of admission to the facility, he maintains the civil rights of any citizen, such as the right to vote, to manage his financial affairs, and to execute legal documents.[2] As a result of the nature of the confinement of a patient in a mental health facility, he or she is guaranteed certain minimal legal rights. The right to consult or communicate with an attorney while hospitalized is considered to be constitutionally required. If the facility attempts to limit the right of a patient to have any visitors, including a lawyer, the position must be therapeutically defensible and well documented. One well-known expert in the field, Bruce Ennis, states that the only justification for denying this right "should be a compelling reason."[3]

Additionally, most states specify that a patient has the right to receive mail without interference or censorship, the right to receive visitors, and the right not to be denied the basic necessities of life in the name of treatment. While these rights may be temporarily restricted under certain circumstances, a mere claim by the staff that interference with these rights is necessary for treatment purposes is insufficient to deny a patient the rights.

One federal court stated that patients had a right to send and receive sealed mail from "attorneys, doctors, mental health professionals, and public officials."⁴ Some states require that the patient "designate correspondents before communicating with them."⁵ *In Davis v. Balson* the court found the following practices unconstitutional in a maximum security hospital in Ohio: "the opening of incoming general correspondence outside the presence of the patient; the practice of reading and censoring outgoing mail from patients that have been the subject of complaints from members of the public."⁶

States vary in defining other legal rights. Almost half the states grant individuals the right to wear their personal belongings. Less than a quarter of the states delineate requirements for storage space for personal possessions.⁷ Anyone who has visited a state hospital ward will have observed that privacy is difficult to attain. Consequently, many states have passed legislation to ensure patients "some degree of personal privacy, autonomy, good health, and dignity."⁸

As stated in a previous chapter, confidentiality of the records of the mentally disabled is imperative. In addition, it is important to keep a complete and accurate record of the individual's course of treatment. Mental health professionals who have worked in state hospitals during the last ten years cannot avoid noting the improvement in record keeping in regard to patients' course of treatment. This is probably due to the increase in numbers of professionals working within the mental health system and the motivation of state systems to ensure that they receive accreditation by the Joint Commission on the Accreditation of Hospitals.

Access To Patient Records

Approximately two-thirds of the states have passed statutes governing the accessibility of patient records.⁹ Release forms should be signed by the patient or guardian before a professional disseminates information about the patient to anyone. Some community mental health centers are not part of the state hospital system; therefore release forms should be obtained before sharing patient data. This should be accomplished in a timely manner so that continuity of patient care is maintained.

Review of Patient Records

Almost half the states require periodic review of the patient's condition to determine if he continues to meet the standard for hospitalization.¹⁰ Tennessee allows a patient to consult with a licensed physician practicing outside the hospital. If the person is indigent, the state system will provide the remuneration.[11] Since a person's condition is subject to change even after long periods of hospitalization, review of the patient's treatment plan should be routine. Ennis proposes that periodic judicial review be constitutionally required and recommends that judicial review of confined patients take place every six months.[12]

Least Restrictive Alternative

The concept of least restrictive alternative was discussed previously with emphasis on when to hospitalize a person. Least restrictive alternative applies within the hospital setting as well. During hospitalization, a change in a patient's condition may warrant a revision in the treatment plan; therefore treatment regimens should be frequently evaluated. Mechanisms to transfer a client efficiently from one alternative to another should be developed.[13] Adequate documentation to justify changing should be present, particularly when the patient is being transferred to a more restrictive setting, because such a modification could be judicially reviewed.

Seclusion and Restraints

A substantial number of states have laws specifying and restricting the use of restraints and seclusion. The major guideline is that the restraint can be used only to prevent serious harm to the patients or others in the immediate environment.[14] Seclusion practices were a major issue in the Massachusetts case of *Rogers v. Okin.* Although the court held that seclusion practices at Boston State Hospital had been utilized as a form of treatment and not as punishment, in some instances of isolation no "serious threat of extreme violence, personal injury, or attempted suicide" existed.[15] Therefore, seclusion should be based on whether the patient is harmful to himself or others. In the landmark case *Wyatt v. Stickney,* the court ruled:

> Patients have a right to be free from physical restraint and isolation. Except for emergency situations, in which it is likely that patients could harm themselves or others and in which less restrictive means of restraint are not feasible, patients may be physically restrained or placed in isolation only on a Qualified Health Professional's written order which explains the rationale for such action. The written order may be entered only after the

Qualified Mental Health Professional has personally seen the patient concerned and evaluated whatever episode or situation is said to call for restraint or isolation. Emergency use of restraints or isolation shall be for no more than one hour, by which time a Qualified Mental Health Professional shall have been consulted and shall have entered an appropriate order in writing. Such written order shall be effective for no more than 24 hours and must be renewed if restraint and isolation are to be continued. While in restraint or isolation the patient must be seen by qualified ward personnel who will chart the patient's physical condition (if it is compromised) and psychiatric condition every hour. The patient must have bathroom privileges every hour and must be bathed every 12 hours.[16]

Nursing Implications. Nurses should be familiar with the rules and regulations promulgated by the health care facility in which they work relative to seclusion of patients. Although it is sometimes necessary to seclude patients for their own and others' safety, this is an extraordinary deprivation of liberty. Documentation of the precipitating event that warranted seclusion, as well as alternatives attempted or considered, should be included in the patient's record. Recording of the patient's behavior during seclusion is important. The patient should be checked frequently, and continuing periods of seclusion should be carefully evaluated. Seclusion of patients has become subject to litigation recently. The nurse should be forewarned that seclusion of patients must be therapeutically indicated and justified.

Inpatient Work

Several suits have been filed by patients concerning work in an institution. Some states provide for compensation at the minimum wage or higher.[17] The key element seems to be that patients should not be performing work that involves the continuing maintenance and operation of the hospital without remuneration. Ordinary tasks such as cleaning up around the patient's own bedside unit or housekeeping tasks on the ward do not require payment.[18]

In a consent order entered in *Schindenwolf v. Klein,* the following guideline was promulgated: "All work performed for which the institution should otherwise have to pay an employee shall be compensated."[19] The remuneration would have to be commensurate with that given to persons in the community, with the exception that it could be adjusted if the resident's disability inhibited his performance of the work.[20]

Payment for Hospitalization

Almost all jurisdictions require patients or their families to pay for the expense of hospitalization. This pertains to voluntary as well as involuntary patients.[21] Recent cases have reinforced and reaffirmed this doctrine. In Pennsylvania, parents of an incompetent 28-year-old man were required to pay the cost of his hospitalization in a state facility.[22] In another decision, an Oklahoma court concluded that collection of an unpaid $5000 was recoverable from the estate of a patient.[23]

Right to Treatment

In 1970, a group of employees from Bryce Hospital in Tuscaloosa, Alabama lost their jobs as a result of an impending deficit in the mental health department budget.

In October, 1971, a class action suit was filed in the United States District Court for the Middle District of Alabama on behalf of the employees and patients of Bryce Hospital; Ricky Wyatt, a patient on the adolescent unit and a relative of one of the employees, was named as plaintiff.[24]

The attorney for the plaintiffs set forth the premise that the dismissal of the employees would result in a lower standard of care and that patients had a constitutional right to treatment.[25] He acknowledged the contribution of a law student who developed the idea based on a law-review article which discussed the decision of *Rouse v. Cameron*.[26] The latter case involved an individual found not guilty by reason of insanity. He was committed to a federal mental health facility. Judge David Bazelon ruled that institutionalized persons had a right to treatment, but this particular decision was based on a District of Columbia statute that delineated this right. Judge Frank M. Johnson, Jr. declined to hear the case related to the labor dispute but consented to consider the constitutional question of right to treatment.

In subsequent rulings, Judge Johnson stated that patients did have a right to treatment. In one of the rulings concerning Bryce Hospital, he discussed the conditions at the facility. He commented that the "barnlike" dormitories afforded no privacy and that no space was set aside for individual patients to call their own. The admissions procedure was demeaning and humiliating, and could cause a patient to form an impression of the hospital as a "prison or crazy house." Only 50¢ a day was spent on food for each patient, and the common sanitation procedure utilized at other hospitals was not followed at Bryce Hospital. It was a dehumanizing situation.[27] Some of the standards of care set forth by Judge Johnson for the operation of Bryce Hospital follow:

Patients have a right to privacy and dignity.

Patients have a right to the least restrictive conditions necessary to achieve the purposes of commitment.

Patients shall have the same rights to visitation and telephone communication as patients at other public hospitals, except to the extent that the Qualified Mental Health Professional responsible for formulation of a particular patient's treatment plan writes an order imposing special restrictions. The written order must be renewed after periodic review of the treatment plan if any restrictions are to be continued. Patients shall have an unrestricted right to visitation with attorneys and with private physicians and other health professionals.

Patients shall have an unrestricted right to send sealed mail. Patients shall have an unrestricted right to receive sealed mail from their attorneys, private physicians, and other mental health professionals, from courts, and government officials. Patients shall have a right to receive sealed mail from others, except to the extent that the Qualified Mental Health Professional responsible for formulation of a particular patient's treatment plan writes an order imposing special restrictions on receipt of sealed mail. The written order must be reviewed after each periodic review of the treatment plan if any restrictions are to be continued.

Patients have a right to wear their own clothes and to keep and use their own personal possessions except insofar as such clothes or personal possessions may be determined by a Qualified Mental Health Professional to be dangerous or otherwise inappropriate to the treatment regimen.

Each patient shall have a comprehensive physical and mental

examination and review of behavioral status within 48 hours after admission to the hospital.

Each patient shall have an individualized treatment plan. This plan shall be developed by appropriate Qualified Mental Health Professionals, including a psychiatrist, and implemented as soon as possible—in any event no later than five days after the patient's admission. Each individualized treatment plan shall contain:
a. a statement of the nature of the specific problems and specific needs of the patient;
b. a statement of the least restrictive treatment conditions necessary to achieve the purposes of commitment;
c. a description of intermediate and long-range treatment goals, with a projected timetable for their attainment;
d. a statement and rationale for the plan of treatment for achieving these intermediate and long-range goals;
e. a specification of staff responsibility and a description of proposed staff involvement with the patient in order to attain these treatment goals;
f. criteria for release to less restrictive treatment conditions.[28]

Wyatt v. Stickney was subsequently upheld by the Fifth Circuit Court of Appeals in 1974.[29] Almost ten years after the initial suit was filed, the state of Alabama was placed in receivership for failure to comply with the standards. The governor of Alabama was made receiver of the system, and a monitor was appointed to scrutinize compliance.[30] The effect of this decision nationwide has been enormous. Flowing from this decision is a phenomenal amount of litigation and legislation which has markedly affected hospitalized patients' rights.[31]

In a more recent United States Supreme Court case, *O'Connor v. Donaldson*, it was ruled that the state cannot hospitalize a nondangerous person in a mental institution against his will without treatment if he is capable of surviving safely in the community with a support system of friends and family.[32] Mr. Donaldson, diagnosed as paranoid schizophrenic, had been hospitalized more than 14 years in a mental institution in Florida. After his first examination, Mr. Donaldson, a Christian Scientist, declined to take medication or any other treatment, such as electroconvulsive therapy. He was confined in a locked room with about 60 other patients. One-third of these individuals were criminals. When Mr. Donaldson asked for grounds privileges and occupational therapy, his requests were rejected. One of his former college classmates offered to take him into his home in New York State, but these requests were denied by the hospital administration. At no time was there evidence that Mr. Donaldson was in a therapeutic milieu, although the hospital described it as such. This premise was rejected by the court.[33] This is a very limited decision and is not as encompassing a ruling as *Wyatt v. Stickney*, a lower court decision that affects only those states in the Fifth Circuit.

Behavioral Modification

Behavior therapies implemented for the treatment of the mentally ill and residents of prisons have varied widely. Most nurses are familiar with token economy, in which an individual can earn tokens or privileges based on positive behavior as outlined by the staff. Other more intrusive methods have also been used in an attempt to change patients' behavior. The following case is an example.

In *Knecht v. Gillman*, residents of the Iowa Security Medical Facility filed suit alleging cruel and unusual punishment. This institution provided treatment for individuals who needed mental health services in a secure setting. The residents alleged that injections of apomorphine were given to them without consent and that this practice constituted cruel and unusual punishment, in violation of the Eighth Amendment. Apomorphine was given as an aversive treatment to manage behavior problems of the residents. It was not clear whether or not informed consent was secured; however, if an inmate did consent to the procedure, revocation of the consent was not permitted. A behavior protocol was established for the individual by the staff. Behaviors for which a resident received apomorphine included: not getting up out of bed, giving cigarettes against orders, talking, swearing, and lying. Other inmates or staff would report breach of the protocol, and a nurse would give the injection. The staff did not have to observe the violation themselves for the medication to be given.

The hypodermic injection was given, and the individual was exercised fifteen minutes before he began vomiting. Vomiting usually continued fifteen minutes to one hour. The physiologic changes associated with administration of apomorphine include changes in blood pressure and in functioning of the heart. The court, after reviewing the facts, stated that forcing an individual to vomit for a minor infraction of the rules could only be regarded as cruel and unusual punishment, unless the person "knowingly and intelligently has consented to it."[34] The court issued the following rules: If the procedure was to continue, written consent and certification by a physician was necessary, and the patient must know and understand all the terms of the agreement. The consent could be revoked at any time. Each injection had to be authorized by a physician and administered by a doctor or nurse. The staff had to observe personally the unacceptable behavior which could result in administration of medication. Even though the court ruled that this procedure could be utilized with these specific guidelines, one might question whether this particular form of behavior modification should be considered as a possible treatment. Rosoff comments on the coercive atmosphere of this particular situation.[35]

Nursing Implications. To ensure that a patient's rights are not violated, it is important to be familiar with institutional or departmental guidelines. The more intrusive the procedure, the greater the need for informed consent. Martin sets forth comprehensive checklists that would be useful to review before starting such a program.[36] These include questions to be addressed before obtaining informed consent; goal setting; effectiveness evaluation; supervision and control; and written documentation.

Research on the Mentally Ill

Institutional Review Boards (IRB) were created by the Federal Government to prevent violation of patients' rights for projects funded by the federal government. The major thrust of the guidelines is to ensure informed consent, and to guarantee that the risks to the patient are outweighed by the potential benefits. The knowledge to be gained from the project should warrant allowing the subject to accept the risks.[37] Many institutions adopted guidelines permitting review boards to peruse all research to be performed that utilized human subjects, even projects not funded by the federal government. In 1978, the National Commission for the Protection of Human Subjects of Biomedical and Behavior Research developed some recommendations for research involving the mentally infirm who are institutionalized.[38]

Nursing Implications. It is important for nurses working on units where research is being conducted to be certain that the researchers have gone through the proper channels to have the research approved.

It is also imperative that nurse researchers be cognizant of the procedure for approval of research within their own institution as well as within the agency or facility in which they plan to conduct the research.

Right to Aftercare

Many articles have been written in professional and lay literature about some of the deplorable conditions faced by deinstitutionalized mental patients upon leaving the hospital. Article titles vividly depict the situation. "Out of Their Beds and Into the Streets" and "Health Care's Dumping Ground" characterize the plight of the chronically mentally disabled in the community.[39] One author describes some former mental patients as "ragtag figures seen huddled in doorways."[40] In 1977, public hearings were held across the country by the President's Commission on Mental Health. During these sessions, individuals testified to the lack of aftercare services and the fragmentation of care.

Reports have indicated that only 10% to 30% of discharged mental hospital patients acquire employment; exacerbations of the illness and rehospitalization rates range from 35% to 50% in the first year after discharge, and 65% to 75% within five years.[41] Fragmentation and disorganization of service delivery are frequently mentioned as causes. Lamb recommends that a variety of community living arrangements be established and given financial support. This will not be inexpensive, but unless the underfunding of programs ceases, "We will continue to provide deplorable conditions for our severely mentally ill, and the 'shame of the states' will simply have been moved to the community."[42]

In *Dixon v. Weinberger*, the court stated that patients should be placed in the least restrictive alternative, and that solutions to the problems of placing patients in these situations must be submitted.[43] A consent decree in *Brewster v. Dukakis* stipulated "that community programs would have to be upgraded, and alternatives created where none existed."[44] Saphire contends in a law review article that aftercare is a constitutional right. This issue has not been ruled upon by the courts, but all mental health professionals should attempt to provide continuity of care as well as adequate planning for the patient's continued care upon discharge from the hospital.[45]

Advocacy

Some states have developed advocacy projects within mental health facilities in their system. The purpose of advocacy is not only to ensure that the legal rights of the patients are protected, but also to improve the quality of the day-to-day life of patients in the institutional setting. The Federal Mental Health Systems Act of 1980 originally provided federal support for such programs, but this was repealed.[46] Advocates assist patients in maintaining their rights. Kopolow states that patients have "the right not to be psychiatric patients." He continues that patients today are more likely to be assertive and less apt to be passive recipients of care.[47] Many patients' rights groups organized in the last ten years throughout the country are currently setting forth their views on mental health care.

Written statements regarding patients' rights may have a limited impact on the life of the patient or the quality of care provided to him. At least three areas of advocacy can be identified that would maximize the fulfillment of patients' rights: (1) to educate and train the facility staff properly and to implement policies and procedures that recognize and protect patients' rights; (2) to establish an additional procedure to permit the speedy resolution of problems, questions, or disagreements that occur and that may or may not be based on legal rights; and (3) to provide access to legal services when a patient's legal right has been denied. The third area usually requires an advocate who is not employed by the facility but is located at the facility.

Although many mental health professionals applaud the advocacy movement, one author has expressed concern about advocates who create a situation in which the mental health professional and the advocate are placed in an adversary position for long periods, leading to mutual suspicion and subsequent poor and fragmented care. Lamb suggests that advocates should be required to receive in-depth education concerning the nature of mental illness. Following this educational experience, direct service should be provided by the advocates to very disturbed patients within a psychiatric facility.[48] This would give the advocates perspective on the treatment of psychiatric patients. Some might argue, however, that advocates would lose their objectivity if this process took place routinely.

If an advocate is present within a mental health care system, his role should be carefully outlined by administrators in order to avoid confusion among the staff giving care. Kopolow recommends that psychiatrists advocate treatment alternatives to hospitalization and support changes in the laws when needed.[49] For nurses who have traditionally attempted to ensure that patients are granted their rights, careful thought must be given to the delivery of nursing care and to advocating changes that would allow improvement of care.

In a recent study by the *Mental Disability Law Reporter*, state statutes were surveyed to determine whether the laws actually protected patients' rights. Originally, the Mental Health Systems Act outlined a patient's bill of rights. This bill was deleted, based on the assumption that states already had laws providing for rights. The assumption proved to be false. Only five states complied with half the act's recommendations; only 22 states complied with one-third of the recommendations.[50]

Nursing Implications. Nurses should be aware of the basic rights of mental health patients as established within the mental health care system. If certain basic rights are delineated in statutes or outlined in case law, mechanisms should be in place within a health care facility to guarantee those rights. If a nurse observes violation of patients' rights, the incidents should be reported to an administrator. Nurses must stay informed through continuing education programs and by reading material that outlines legislative and judicial changes in the law. Because of the number of registered professional nurses in each state, political power bases for influencing passage of legislation that guarantees protection of patients' rights can be established.

REFERENCES

1. Rights of Disabled Persons in Residential Facilities. Mental Disability Law Reporter, vol. 3, no. 5, 1979, pp. 348–365.
2. Ibid.
3. Bruce Ennis and Richard D. Emery: The Rights of Mental Patients, An American Civil Liberties Union Handbook. New York, Avon Books, 1978, p. 154.
4. *Wyatt v. Stickney*, 344 F. Supp. 373 at 379
5. Rights of Disabled Persons in Residential Facilities, p. 349.
6. *Davis v. Balson*, 461 F. Supp. 842 (W.D. Ohio, 1978).
7. Rights of Disabled Persons in Residential Facilities, p. 348.
8. Ibid.
9. Ibid.
10. Ibid., pp. 357–359.
11. Tennessee Code Annotated, Section 33-609.
12. Ennis: Rights of Mental Patients, p. 128.
13. Reed Martin: Workshop Materials: Legal Challenges in Regulating Behavior Change. Public Law Div. Champaign, IL, Research Press Company, 1979, p. 27.

14. Rights of Disabled Persons in Residential Facilities, p. 348.
15. *Rogers v. Okin,* 478 F. Supp. 1342 at 1374, (1979). Also, *Rogers v. Okin,* 634 F2d 650 (1980).
16. *Wyatt v. Stickney,* 344 F. Supp. 373 at 380.
17. Rights of Disabled Persons in Residential Facilities, pp. 360-362.
18. California Patient Labor Case Settled. Mental Disability Law Reporter, 5: 187.
19. Expansive Work Program Outlined for New Jersey Psychiatric Patients. Mental Disability Law Reporter, 5: 60-61.
20. Ibid.
21. Ennis: Rights of Mental Patients, p. 156.
22. *Lansing v. Pennsylvania Department of Public Welfare,* 410 A2d 982 (1980).
23. *Oklahoma v. Storer,* 614 P2d 59 (1980).
24. *Wyatt v. Stickney:* Retrospect and Prospect. Hospital and Community Psychiatry, vol. 32, no. 2, February 1981, p. 123 at 124.
25. Carole W. Offir: Civil Rights and the Mentally Ill: Revolution in Bedlam. Psychology Today, October 1974, p. 61.
26. *Rouse v. Cameron,* 373 F2d 451 (D.C. Circuit 1957).
27. *Wyatt v. Stickney,* 334 F. Supp. 1341 at 1343 (1971).
28. *Wyatt v. Stickney,* 344 F. Supp. 373, 379-384 (1972).
29. *Wyatt v. Aderholt,* 503 F2d 1305 (Fifth Circuit 1974).
30. *Wyatt v. Stickney:* Retrospect and Prospect. Hospital and Community Psychiatry, p. 125.
31. Harry C. Schnibne: How the States Have Met the Challenge, "10 Years After." Paper presented at the Symposium on *Wyatt v. Stickney* Case, Tuscaloosa, Alabama, September 25-26, 1980.
32. *O'Connor v. Donaldson,* 422 U.S. 563 (1975).
33. *Donaldson v. O'Connor,* 493 F2d 507 (Fifth Circuit 1974).
34. *Knecht v. Gillman,* 488 F2d 1136 at 1139 (Eighth Circuit 1973).
35. Arnold J. Rosoff: Informed Consent. Rockville, MD, Aspen Systems Corporation, 1981, p. 234.
36. Martin: Workshop Materials, pp. 110-115.
37. George J. Annas, Leonard H. Glantz, and Barbara F. Katz: The Rights of Doctors, Nurses and Allied Health Professionals. New York, Avon Books, 1981, p. 142.
38. Protection of Human Subjects, Research Involving those Institutionalized as Mentally Infirm; Report and Recommendations for Public Comment. Federal Register, 43: 11328-11358.
39. Henry Santiestevan: Out of Their Beds and Into the Streets, Washington, D.C., American Federation of State and County Employees, December 1976. Also, Samantha G. Johnson: Health Care's Dumping Ground. The Boston Globe Magazine, May 30, 1982, pp. 7, 14, 16-20.
40. Johnson: Dumping Ground, p. 14.
41. W.A. Anthony, M.R. Cohen, and R. Vitulo: The Measurement of Rehabilitation Outcome. Schizophrenia Bulletin, vol. 4, no. 3, 1978, pp. 365-383. Also H. Richard Lamb: What Did We Really Expect from Deinstitutionalization? Hospital and Community Psychiatry, vol. 32, no. 2, February 1981, pp. 105-109.

42. Lamb: What Did We Expect, p. 109.
43. *Dixon v. Weinberger,* 405 F. Supp. 974 (D.C. 1975).
44. Martin: Workshop Materials, p. 131.
45. R.B. Saphire: The Civilly Committed Public Mental Patient and the Right to Aftercare. Florida State University Law Review, 4:232.
46. Mental Health Systems Act of 1980, Publ. No. 96-398, 94 Stat 1564 (1980).
47. Louis E. Kopolow: Consumer Demands in Mental Health Care. International Journal of Law and Psychiatry, vol. 2, 1979, pp. 263-270, at 269.
48. H. Richard Lamb: Securing Patient's Rights—Responsibly. Hospital and Community Psychiatry, vol. 32, no. 6, June 1981, pp. 393-397.
49. Kopolow: Consumer Demands, pp. 263-270.
50. Martha A. Lyon, Martha L. Levine, and Jack Zusman; Patient's Bill of Rights: A Survey of State Statutes, Mental Disability Law Reporter, 6: 178-201, at 179.

CHAPTER 5
The Right To Refuse Treatment

In recent years, there has been a proliferation of lawsuits concerning the right to refuse treatment, especially involving psychotropic drugs. Many states have guidelines for the administration of electroconvulsive therapy (ECT) and psychosurgery; however, the controversy over refusal of medication is a more recent occurrence. Because the right to refuse treatment has received much attention, an entire chapter is devoted to the issue.

ECT and psychosurgery are performed by physicians, but nurses should be informed about recent court decisions relating to pharmacotherapy because they are primarily responsible for the actual administration of medications. Administration of psychotropic medication is problematic because the United States Supreme Court has not resolved the issue, and many state statutes still permit the involuntary administration of medication. The nurse probably will be the first person confronted with the patient's refusal of medication. The following discussions concern the major cases related to medication refusal. The cases are reported in depth because of the controversy surrounding their rulings.

Rennie v. Klein

John Rennie, an involuntary patient at Ancora Psychiatric Hospital in New Jersey, filed a complaint in December 1977 seeking an injunction to enjoin (an order to stop) the psychiatrists and officials at Ancora from forcibly medicating him without a presenting emergency situation. Mr. Rennie, a highly intelligent former pilot and flight instructor, was involuntarily committed to Ancora.[1] He had a history of many hospitalizations in public and private facilities beginning in 1973 following the death of his twin brother in an airplane accident.

During Mr. Rennie's confinement in the hospital, physicians had been unable to arrive at a precise diagnosis of his condition. Some doctors identified the schizophrenic process; others concluded he suffered from manic depression. There was also no consensus concerning the appropriate medication to be given to him.

Symptoms exhibited during his illness included delusions, aggressive behavior with homicidal threats, and suicidal gestures. During the admission that prompted the initial lawsuit, he was placed in a unit described as a "barren, bleak ward."[2] He had long periods of unproductive, unplanned time with infrequent contact with physicians, although such contact increased after the lawsuit was filed. Before the lawsuit, even though his condition had been deteriorating, he still refused to take medication. After the facility consulted with and was granted permission by the Attorney General's office, he was given medication without his consent. Injectable Prolixin was selected because of its long-lasting effect; the need for administration occurred once every two weeks. It was considered an ideal treatment modality because of Rennie's previous nonconformance with medication regimens upon discharge. Subsequently he filed the lawsuit and the request for an injunction.

Mr. Rennie developed side effects from Thorazine or Prolixin. He suffered from akasthesia (an inability to be still), uncontrollable tremors, and wormlike movements of the tongue, which might have indicated tardive dyskinesia. Prominent symptoms of tardive dyskinesia are "face and neck movements including chewing, smacking and licking of the lips, sucking, tongue protrusions, tongue tremor with open mouth, wormlike movements on the surface of the tongue, blinking, and facial distortions."[3] The condition "has been found to be irreversible in some patients."[4] For these reasons, Mr. Rennie did not want to take the medication.

The court ruled that based on the right of privacy, mental patients in nonemergency situations could refuse treatment. However, it is a qualified right, taking into account the following factors: the patient's threat of physical harm to other persons, the patient's capacity to make decisions for himself, the existence and availability of less restrictive treatment, and the risk of permanent side effects to the individual.

Because Mr. Rennie was no longer receiving involuntary administration of Prolixin, an injunction was not issued at the time of the first court hearing. Later in 1978 Mr. Rennie returned to court again seeking an injunction, this time to halt the administration of Thorazine against his will. In an opinion issued in December 1978, the court decided that based on his current behavior, Mr. Rennie did not have the capacity to make decisions concerning the intake of drugs and that the least restrictive treatment at that time was medication.[5]

In 1979, another lawsuit was filed by Mr. Rennie for injunctive relief against hospitals and staffs to prevent forcible administration of drugs. The lawsuit was expanded to a class action which included:

persons currently hospitalized or those who might be hospitalized in the future at Ancora Psychiatric Hospital, involuntarily committed patients of the five mental health facilities operated by the Division of Mental Health and Hospitals in New Jersey, and voluntary patients residing in the five facilities.[6]

A procedure had been outlined in an administrative bulletin issued in March 1978 by the Division of Mental Health Hospitals for handling patients who refused to take prescribed medication. Under this procedure, voluntary patients had a right to refuse medication. However, if an involuntary patient refused, the physician was required first to inform the patient about his condition and then describe the risks and benefits of the drugs to be given, including any other available alternative treatments. If the patient still refused, the treatment team was to review the issue. The team included nurses, social workers, psychologists, and the treating physician. The finding of the team was used only as a recommendation to the treating physician, who had the ultimate responsibility for prescribing drugs.

Patients who were legally competent could have their cases reviewed by the medical director of the hospital. Before authorizing the involuntary administration of medication, the medical director was required to conduct a personal examination of the patient. An independent psychiatrist could be consulted if desired. The medical director was then required to review the treatment program of the patient each week that patient protested the administration of involuntary medication. The patient could request that an attorney be present during this process.

If a patient found incompetent by the court refused medication, the guardian would be consulted. If the treatment team disagreed with the physician, either the medical director or his designee would examine the patient. If this physician agreed with the prior opinions, consent of the guardian would again be sought. If the guardian did not consent, the chief executive officer could consent.

In March 1979, an additional review procedure was added. Physicians in the central office of the Division of Mental Health and Hospitals were authorized to review further authorization of the use of involuntary medication. At the time of the hearing, only two patients' records, including that of Mr. Rennie, had been reviewed. The court found that this was not a regular procedure that patients could trust.

In making its decision, the court relied upon the examples of several patients and their refusals to take medications. One example was a

23-year-old female patient who testified in the case and whose demeanor impressed the judge. While a patient, she became pregnant and openly resisted taking medication because she did not want to harm the baby.[7] The physician continued to prescribe Haldol, a psychotropic drug. The patient complained to the Public Advocate's office, which interceded, but the hospital medical director did not change the order. Subsequently, she ingested some detergent and was transferred to the medical unit of the hospital. The drug was then discontinued because her diagnosis did not warrant the use of psychotropics. She began to do small chores on the ward, and her condition improved to the extent that she was discharged two months after admission to the medical unit.[8]

After hearing the evidence in the case, the federal district court ruled that patients had constitutional rights of privacy and due process while involuntarily committed. The court further held that the following procedures, which apply to psychotropic medication only, should be adopted. All patients, voluntary or involuntary, have to sign consent forms to be used in all nonemergency situations, except when the patient has been declared legally or functionally incompetent. (*Legally incompetent* indicates that a court has adjudicated the individual unable to manage his affairs. *Functionally incompetent* means that a physician has determined that the individual cannot make a medication decision for himself.) There must be information about the drugs and their side effects contained in the forms. Also, patient advocates would be required to analyze those cases in which patients were considered incompetent to make an informed decision about medication. The advocate could enlist inhospital and independent review of the medication order. Advocates would also serve as informal counsel to patients who refused their medications.

An informal review by an independent psychiatrist would be required before the hospital could forcibly medicate an involuntary patient. It was the belief of the court that a psychiatrist would be more effective than a judge, an attorney, or a layperson. During an emergency situation, both voluntary and involuntary patients could be medicated to prevent harm.

> The court holds that the qualified privacy right is always outweighed in these emergency situations where the patient is in an acute psychotic state, has little competence but often is in great need of a psychotropic drug, and short-term use presents very little risk of permanent side effects.[9]

The New Jersey State Hospital officials appealed the decision. In 1981, the Third Circuit United States Court of Appeals ruled that the administration of psychotropic medication to involuntarily committed patients not adjudicated incompetent must be the least restrictive means of treatment. The court, however, stated that it was not necessary to have an adversary hearing before an independent psychiatrist, as outlined by the federal court judge. The court further held that the procedures instituted by the Division of Mental Health and Hospitals did satisfy due process.

Rennie v. Klein was appealed and was reviewed by the United States Supreme Court in a one-sentence opinion, and was remanded to the Third Circuit Court of Appeals in light of the recent decision *Youngberg v. Romeo*. While the Youngberg case involved issues related to the institutionalization of a mentally retarded individual, the Supreme Court opinion analyzed certain rights of institutionalized persons that apparently apply to the mentally ill as well. The court refused to rule on whether or not a right to minimally adequate habilitation existed, but it recognized that if habilitation was necessary in order to protect the person's safety and freedom from restraints, it was constitutionally required. Since the Supreme Court remanded *Rennie* with instructions to review it in light of this decision, it must be assumed that this approach will be applied to the right to treatment.[10]

Rogers v. Okin

Rogers v. Okin was initially filed in April 1975 as a class action civil rights suit under a federal statute.[11] In this action, the plaintiffs sought to enjoin Boston State Hospital in Massachusetts from specific seclusion and medication practices, and monetary damages were sought. The class action suit was brought by seven patients involuntarily committed to Boston State Hospital against the Commissioner of Mental Health, thirteen physicians, and one individual with a doctorate in counseling. The alleged grievance was forcing patients to submit to medication and seclusion in violation of state and federal law. A temporary restraining order was issued in April 1975 prohibiting nonemergency seclusion and involuntary medication of voluntary and involuntary patients. If a person was adjudicated incompetent, the guardian could give consent.

After the filing of many motions, the trial began in December 1977; it involved 72 trial days. The opinion of the federal district court was issued on October 29, 1979. Judge Tauro ruled that patients had been secluded in nonemergency situations in violation of the state statute that provided for seclusion only in emergency situations "where there is the occurrence of (or) serious threat of extreme violence, personal injury or attempted suicide."[12]

The major controversy, however, centered on the issue of a patient's right to refuse forced medication. The defendants presented the argument that involuntarily committed patients should automatically be considered incompetent when refusing medication. The court rejected this premise and ruled that a patient was presumed to be legally competent to make treatment decisions unless he had been specifically adjudicated otherwise. An involuntary patient who refused medication could only be forced to take drugs if a legally appointed guardian consented to their administration or if an emergency situation existed. Voluntary patients had a right to refuse treatment, and the only instance in which they could be medicated against their will was an emergency situation in which substantial likelihood of physical harm to the patient or others existed.[13]

The court based the right to refuse treatment on an individual's right to privacy and on the First Amendment right to protection of the communication of ideas.

> It is clear from the evidence in this case that psychotropic medication has the potential to affect and change a patient's mood, attitude and capacity to think. Whatever powers the constitution has granted our government, involuntary mind control is not one of them, absent extraordinary circumstances.[14]

The court found the defendants not liable for negligence because the resources available to them were not within their control. "It would be unjust and unreasonable to hold psychiatrists personally and individually responsible for resource deficiencies that are actually the 'responsibility of society.'"[15] In regard to the informed consent of patients taking medication, the court stated that lack of this was not considered below the medical standard of care in 1973 to 1975.

Current Conclusions

The *Rogers* court and the *Rennie* court both used the right of privacy as a basis for the right to refuse treatment. However, the First Amendment right to protection of communication of ideas was used by the judge in the *Rogers* decision only. This ruling was criticized because it seemed to leave most of the decision-making concerning medication of involuntary patients to guardians and judges rather than to psychiatrists. Others hailed the *Rogers* decision as a major victory for the rights of patients movement.[16]

The *Rogers* decision was appealed to the First Circuit Court of Appeals, who rendered their findings in November 1980. The District Court and the Court of Appeals agreed that patients have a right to refuse antipsychotic medications.[17] The Court of Appeals based its ruling on the due process clause of the Fourteenth Amendment "as part of the penumbral right to privacy, bodily integrity or personal security."[18] Since the Court of Appeals believed that the constitutional right to privacy was a sufficient basis for the right to refuse treatment, the court found it unnecessary to decide whether the District Court was correct in finding that "the First Amendment rights of the plaintiffs were abridged by forcibly treating them with antipsychotic drugs."[19]

The Appeals Court ruled that dangerous patients could be medicated against their will. However, it found that the phrase "substantial likelihood of serious harm" lacked flexibility in implementation. The court concluded that the treating professionals must weigh the patient's interests versus the need to prevent violence, balance the risk of harm with the effect that the drugs might have on the patient, and explore reasonable alternatives to the administration of medication. The Court of Appeals ordered that on remand, the District Court should set up procedural mechanisms, including an independent monitoring system, to provide for overseeing the medicating of potentially violent patients against their will.

The Court of Appeals affirmed the District Court's decision regarding adjudication of an incompetent patient by the court. This, of course, can be a lengthy process. Consequently, the Court of Appeals ruled that a guardian did not have to be appointed if a delay could result in significant deterioration of the patient's mental health.[20] The Appeals Court stated that treatment decisions should be made as the individual himself would have desired if he were competent to make that decision, and it instructed the District Court to develop procedures to ensure that the decision makers applied this substituted judgment test.[21]

Voluntary patients do have the right to refuse treatment, but the Court of Appeals stated:

The Statute does not guarantee voluntary patients the treatment of their choice. Instead it offers a treatment regimen that state doctors and staff determine is best, and if the patient thinks otherwise, he can leave. We can find nothing even arguably unconstitutional in such a statutory scheme.[22]

Richard Cole, in reviewing the implications of *Rogers*, points out that many state hospital patients are of the lower socioeconomic class, who have nowhere else to go for treatment, and that these individuals might be faced with submitting to an "unwanted treatment or no treatment at all."[23] State institutions are their only treatment options. It is important to point out that voluntary patients who do not accept treatment, and who cannot be released to the community because of their mental condition, should be considered for involuntary commitment.

Recent Developments

The Court of Appeals decision in *Rogers v. Okin* was appealed to the United States Supreme Court, which handed down an opinion in June 1982. It essentially remanded the case back to the Court of Appeals for review, taking into consideration a Massachusetts Supreme Court decision, *In the Matter of Guardianship of Richard Roe, III*, decided five months after the Court of Appeals decision in *Rogers v. Okin*.

Richard Roe III (a pseudonym) was 21 years old and had been diagnosed as having paranoid schizophrenia. He had been treated and hospitalized on two occasions.[24] He was scheduled to be released from a state hospital. Because of his propensity for assaulting others and refusal to take medication, it was determined he needed a temporary guardian. The father was appointed. The probate judge, relying on *Rogers v. Okin*, authorized the temporary guardian to consent to forcible administration of antipsychotic medications. Before the hearing for appointment of a permanent guardian, Roe was released from the hospital.

When the permanent guardianship hearing was convened, the Commissioner of the Massachusetts Department of Mental Health was allowed to become a party to the case, as were the plaintiffs in *Rogers v. Okin*. In July 1980, the probate judge appointed Roe's father as a permanent guardian with the authority to consent to forcible medication. Roe had an aversion to taking medications because of prior illicit drug use which caused him "to be involved in an automobile accident."[25] There was some evidence to indicate he also refused because of his belief in the Christian Science faith.

The Supreme Judicial Court of Massachusetts ruled that in order to guarantee objectivity, the guardian did not have authority to consent to antipsychotic drug treatments without a specific court order. The following factors must be considered before a trial court may authorize administration of involuntary medication.

1. The ward's expressed preferences regarding treatment. Even though the ward may lack the capacity to make treatment decisions, his preference is "entitled to serious consideration as a factor in the substituted judgment determination."[26]

2. The ward's religious beliefs. A person who while competent expressed ideas based on his religion that might affect his willingness to accept or reject a specific treatment should have these beliefs taken into consideration.

3. The impact upon the ward's family. If the person lived at home and was an integral part of a close family, and giving him medication would prevent his being isolated in an institution, this fact must be taken into consideration.[27]

4. The consequences if treatment is refused. The court should determine what the implications of treatment would be for each person, taking into consideration the unique circumstances surrounding the situation.

5. The prognosis with treatment. "We think it can fairly be stated that the greater the likelihood that there will be cure or improvement, the more likely an individual would be to submit to intrusive treatment accompanied by the possibility of adverse side effects."[28] The possible benefits must be weighed along with the feasibility of the person's actually deriving benefit from the treatment. Not all patients respond the same to a prescribed treatment.

The court also ruled that forcible treatment is allowable to protect the public safety, but the likelihood of serious harm must be established beyond a reasonable doubt. The court further held that the less intrusive means of treatment should be utilized; this would be determined by the "means of restraint which would be chosen by the ward if he were competent to choose."[29] The guidelines established by the court applied only in circumstances in which the following factors existed: (1) an incompetent individual is not institutionalized; (2) a party with standing actually seeks to administer medication to the incompetent person in the absence of an emergency, which we define as an unforeseen combination of circumstances or the resulting state that calls for immediate action; and (3) the proposed medication is an antipsychotic drug.[30]

In another article in *Law, Medicine and Health Care*, Cole commented that the *Roe* court relied upon both state and federal law for its decision, and that this would affect the United States Supreme Court's decision. His prediction proved correct as *Rogers v. Okin* was remanded to the Court of Appeals to be reviewed in light of the *Roe* decision. *Rogers v. Okin*, therefore, is still subject to modifications by the Court of Appeals ruling.*

Current State of the Law

Mental health professionals in Massachusetts still do not have the final answer for implementing guidelines when a patient refuses medication. Two authors involved with the Massachusetts mental health system have reported the distress of the staff working in an environment under a restraining order. Dr. Michael J. Gill states that hostility, suspicion, and an adversarial quality entered relationships between patients and staff.[31] Although the federal court's opinion states that only 12 of 1000 patients refused their medications between May 1, 1975 and June 23, 1977, both Dr. Michael Gill and Stephen Schultz dispute this conclusion, citing higher figures.[32,33] They also note that the need to seclude patients increased.

In New Jersey, Alexander Brooks comments, "Despite original resistance, apprehension and short-term problems that required straightening out, psychiatrists and other hospital staff have adjusted well to the modest requirements of *Rennie*."[34] Irwin Perr, however, writes that two patients hospitalized in private facilities in New Jersey incurred extra expenses of more than $30,000 because of the delay in treatment caused by their refusal to take medication, thus necessitating an independent psychiatrist to be brought in by the hospital.[35] Public advocates and attorneys were also brought in, adding to the expense.

Based on the United States Supreme Court's decision to remand *Rennie v. Klein* to the Third Circuit Court of Appeals in light of the

---

* At the time of printing *Mills v. Rogers* had been referred to the Massachusetts Supreme Judicial Court and *Rennie v. Klein* had been vacated to the Third Circuit Court of Appeals. Neither case has been finally decided. (Paul Appelbaum, *Recent Developments in Mental Health Law,* Chicago, I L., June 8, 1983.)

Youngberg decision, it does seem that the court is stating that a professional's treatment-making decisions should be weighed heavily. Because there has been tremendous concern about mental health professionals minimizing the side effects of psychotropic drugs, consumers may struggle with the implications of this decision.

Nursing Implications. Whatever the outcome of the right to refuse treatment suits, the issue is here to stay. Nurses are on the front line in the administration of medications. It is clear that voluntary patients do have the right to refuse medications and should not be forcibly medicated. The nurse must know and understand the guidelines laid down by the courts in the state where he or she is practicing in order to administer medication properly to involuntary patients. While controversy remains about some legal decisions, there are elements of good clinical practice that can be adopted and encouraged by nurses now.

Scott Nelson writes that questions were generated about the administration of medication to patients not only because of basic constitutional questions but also as a result of concern about the adequacy of care and treatment and its documentation in patients' records within state hospitals. He proposes several guidelines to help ameliorate the situation. A recruitment plan should be developed to select professional personnel who meet the quality standards of practice. There should be some form of quality assurance and peer review of practices and procedures. Continuing education programs about psychotropic medications should be provided for hospital staff. A system should be developed to enable patients to participate actively in treatment decisions. There should be "meaningful patient advocacy."[36]

Although there has been a focus on two major cases, emphasis should be placed on the option that a state system or facility can develop its own regulations for administering psychotropic medication. Nurses, of course, would want to have input into the development of these guidelines. Implementation of rules and regulations regarding the administration of medication would hopefully prevent the abuse that leads to the filing of lawsuits.

Thomas Gutheil and Mark J. Mills remind caregivers in psychiatric settings that a reassuring therapeutic relationship is important in working with a drug-refusing patient. "A positive, caring relationship between staff and patient can play a vital role in reversing a treatment refusal."[37] Nurses should not wait for litigation to be filed to become concerned about this issue. The controversy is here, and it is better to spend time writing well-conceived guidelines and implementing them than to plan a defense for a lawsuit.

Electroconvulsive Therapy

Electroconvulsive therapy (ECT) continues to be used throughout the United States. Joseph Morrissey and associates write that the administration of this treatment modality persists as one of the most "heated controversies in psychiatry."[38] Recent data, however, indicate that the use of ECT has diminished substantially in the last few years.[39]

In a study conducted in New York State, Morrissey found that the majority of ECT was administered in private hospitals to middle-aged white women who had depressive components to their illness. In 1977, only eight percent of the individuals receiving ECT were hospitalized in state mental hospitals. The study concluded that although there were probably some cases of contraindicated use of ECT, there was no widespread "pattern of misuse."[40]

A 1980 issue of *Nursing Law and Ethics* contains a nursing student's letter to the journal describing a situation that had been observed. A patient had revoked consent to ECT en route to the procedure. The patient was held against her will, and the ECT was administered. The question presented by the student was whether the procedure had been carried out in a legal manner. The response indicated that patients have a right to revoke consent unless the individual has been adjudicated incompetent and a guardian appointed.[41]

Competent voluntary patients clearly can refuse to submit to ECT.[42] Ennis points out that most states allow for substituted judgment regarding ECT.[43] A report published by the American Psychiatric Association states that if an incompetent patient's relatives are consulted and consent is given, this should be sufficient. "Good faith on the part of the patient's relatives and psychiatrist should be sufficient to ensure that what is being done, and done expeditiously, is in the best interests of the patient."[44]

George Annas writes: "It is a general custom in the medical community to ask for the consent of the next of kin, and some judicial decisions imply that there is some authority vested in the next of kin."[45] He also comments that the only person who can legally make a binding decision for an incompetent person is a guardian. Therefore, it is imperative that state and case law be consulted and reviewed before allowing substituted judgment by a relative prior to administering ECT.

Nursing Implications. It is important to remember that competent voluntary patients have the right to refuse ECT. In fact, some states have statutorily developed guidelines that define this right. However, there should be a policy and procedure within each facility outlining the mechanism to be used when a physician recommends that ECT be given to an incompetent voluntary or involuntary patient. Legal counsel for the facility should help in developing policies and procedures for implementation of the procedure so that they conform to statutes, case law, and rules and regulations that have been promulgated. Patients are entitled to receive adequate information upon which to base a decision regarding ECT, and they also have the right to alter their decision about the procedure up until the time it is administered.

Psychosurgery

"Psychosurgery is defined as a destruction of some region of the brain in order to alleviate severe and otherwise intractable psychiatric disorders."[46] The treatment of physical symptoms resulting from strokes, tumors, or other pathologic disorders is not considered psychosurgery.[47] According to Robert Grimm, the number of psychosurgery procedures has decreased during the 1970s.[48]

Several states, including Oregon and California, have passed statutes regulating the practice of psychosurgery. Since the passage of this legislation in Oregon and California, the practice of psychosurgery has been very limited in these states. A leading psychosurgery case, *Kaimowitz v. Department of Mental Health*, decided by a circuit court in Michigan and not officially reported, generated a great deal of publicity when the decision was rendered. The individual involved had been charged with murder and rape, was labeled a sexual psychopath, and resided in an institution for seventeen years. He was to undergo experimental brain surgery to determine if his behavior could be altered.[49] The court ruled that involuntarily detained individuals could not freely give truly informed consent. If the suggested procedure had been a routine surgical operation rather than an experimental psychosurgical procedure, the outcome might have been different.[50]

Annas advocates allowing competent patients who have been given adequate information and who can give informed consent to agree to psychosurgery, but he favors prohibiting the procedure for all patients who are incapable of making this decision due to mental incompetence.[51] His response to critics who suggest that this would eliminate an alternative for some patients is that it is a risk "well worth running, since the benefit is speculative but the harm produced by involuntary major surgery is not."[52]

Nursing Implications. Psychosurgery is not frequently implemented. In facilities where the procedure is performed, policies and procedures for obtaining informed consent should be written and carried out based on statutory and case law and on any rules and regulations that have been promulgated.

REFERENCES

1. *Rennie v. Klein*, 462 F. Supp. 1131 (N.J. 1978), p. 1135.
2. Ibid., p. 1136.
3. Carol R. Hartman: Pharmacotherapy. In Ann W. Burgess (ed.): Psychiatric Nursing in the Hospital and the Community, 3rd ed. Englewood Cliffs, N.J., 1981, p. 372.
4. Dilop Jeste and Richard J. Wyatt: Tardive Dyskinesia: The Syndrome, Psychiatric Annals, 10:1, January 1980, p. 16.
5. *Rennie v. Klein*, p. 1153.
6. *Rennie v. Klein,* 476 F. Supp. 1294 (D. N.J. 1979), p. 1298.
7. Ibid., p. 1301.
8. Ibid.
9. Ibid., p. 1312.
10. Leslie Scallett, Scallett and Associates, Washington, DC. Phone conversation, October 7, 1982.
11. *Rogers v. Okin*, 478 F. Supp. 1342 (D. Mass. 1979).
12. Ibid., p. 1371.
13. Ibid.
14. Ibid., pp. 1366–1367.
15. Ibid., p. 1385.
16. Daryl Mathews: The Right to Refuse Psychiatric Medication. Medicolegal News, 8:2, April 1980, p. 4. Also, Richard Cole: The Patient's Right to Refuse Anti-Psychotic Drugs: The Court of Appeals Decision in *Rogers v. Okin*. Medicolegal News, 9:1, February 1981, pp. 10–13.
17. *Rogers v. Okin,* 634 F. 2d 650 (1st Cir. 1980).
18. Ibid., p. 653.
19. Cole: The Patient's Right, p. 11.
20. *Rogers v. Okin*, 634 F. 2d 650, ftn. 16, p. 660
21. Ibid., p. 661.
22. Ibid.
23. Cole: The Patient's Right, p. 14.
24. *In the Matter of Guardianship of Richard Roe, III,* 421 N.E. 2d 40.

25. Ibid., p. 44.
26. Ibid., p. 57.
27. Ibid., p. 58.
28. Ibid., pp. 58, 59.
29. Ibid., p. 61, ftn. 25.
30. Ibid., p. 42.
31. Michael J. Gill: Side Effects of a Right to Refuse Treatment Lawsuit: The Boston State Hospital Experience. In Edward Doudera and Judith Swazey (eds.): Refusing Treatment in Mental Health Institutions — Values in Conflict. Ann Arbor, MI, Association of University Programs in Health Administration Press, 1982, p. 82.
32. *Rogers v. Okin,* 478 F. Supp. 1342 at 1369.
33. Stephen Schultz: The Boston State Hospital Case: A Conflict of Civil Liberties and True Liberalism. American Journal of Psychiatry, 139:2, February 1982, pp. 183-188.
34. Alexander D. Brooks: The Constitutional Right to Refuse Anti-Psychotic Medications. Bulletin of the American Academy of Psychiatry and Law, vol. VIII, no. 2, pp. 180-221, at p. 213.
35. Irwin Perr: Effect of the Rennie Decision on Private Hospitalization in New Jersey: Two Case Reports. American Journal of Psychiatry, 138:6, June 1981, pp. 774-778.
36. Scott Nelson: Should There Be a Right to Refuse Treatment? In Doudera and Swazey, Refusing Treatment, pp. 92, 93.
37. Thomas Gutheil and Mark J. Mills: Clinical Approaches with Patients Who Refuse Medication. In Doudera and Swazey, Refusing Treatment, p. 98.
38. Joseph Morrissey, Henry Steadman, and Nancy Burton: A Profile of ECT Recipients in New York State During 1972 and 1977. American Journal of Psychiatry, 138:5, May 1981, p. 618.
39. Ibid., pp. 621, 622.
40. Ibid., p. 622.
41. Mary Annas: Dear Mary. Nursing Law and Ethics, vol. 1, no. 2, February 1980, p. 5.
42. American Psychiatric Association: Electroconvulsive Therapy: Task Force Report 14. Washington, DC, APA, 1978, p. 143.
43. Bruce Ennis and Richard D. Emery: The Rights of Mental Patients (The Revised ACLU Guide to a Mental Patient's Rights). New York, Avon Books, 1978, p. 139.
44. American Psychiatric Association: Electroconvulsive Therapy, p. 143.
45. George J. Annas, Leonard H. Glantz, and Barbara F. Katz: The Rights of Doctors, Nurses and Allied Health Professionals, New York, Avon Books, 1981, p. 79.
46. Elliott Valenstein: Historical Perspective. In The Psychosurgery Debate. San Francisco, W. H. Freeman and Co., 1980, p. 12.
47. Ibid.
48. Robert J. Grimm: Regulation of Psychosurgery. In Elliot Valenstein (ed.): The Psychosurgery Debate. San Francisco, W. H. Freeman and Co., 1980, p. 437.

Chapter Five

49. Francis C. Pizzulli: Psychosurgery Legislation and Case Law, In Valenstein, The Psychosurgery Debate, p. 382.
50. Samuel I. Shuman: The Concept of Informed Consent. In Valenstein, The Psychosurgery Debate, p. 442.
51. George J. Annas: Effective Psychosurgery: The Greater Danger? In Valenstein, The Psychosurgery Debate, p. 503.
52. Ibid

CHAPTER 6
Forensic Issues

Introduction

Forensics can be defined as those mental health services that are provided to persons who are also involved with the criminal justice system, specifically, those services delivered to persons charged with or convicted of crimes or found to be not guilty by reason of insanity. Traditionally, forensic services have been limited to: (1) inpatient *evaluation* of pretrial defendants to assess competency to stand trial and insanity at the time of the crime; (2) inpatient *treatment* of persons determined by the court to be incompetent to stand trial or not guilty by reason of insanity; and (3) services to persons convicted of crimes and placed in correctional facilities. However, as the result of court decisions in the 1970s, these services were expanded in a number of states to include outpatient evaluation and treatment. Overall, the changes required by the courts in forensic mental health services appear more dramatic than in any other area of mental health. However, because of the history of abuses in the forensic area, the long-term impact has been more limited.

Newspaper exposés have kept the public informed about the abuses and problems that have occurred in both the judicial commitment of mental patients and the routine criminal justice process. As a result of these abuses, substantial changes were made in the criminal procedures and in the judicial commitment procedures. However, few people are acquainted with the double stigma of persons who are labeled as being both mentally ill and a criminal. Although the procedure for commitment of the mentally ill or the resolution of criminal charges may have been imperfect, even these procedural protections were denied those accused or convicted of a crime who were also determined to be mentally ill.

The primary explanation for the different set of procedures used for forensic patients was the theory that they posed a special danger to the public, and the justification for the distinction was the treatment provided to them. Unfortunately, the denial of due process to forensic patients frequently resulted in the lifelong detention of persons who were neither mentally ill nor convicted of a crime; or the detention of persons who, even if mentally ill or guilty of a crime, were held far beyond the maximum sentence they could have received had they actually been found guilty of the crime of which they were accused.

Additionally, the privileges and services available to persons detained in "Asylums for the Criminally Insane" were generally far inferior to those available in prisons.

Although the United States Supreme Court has now drastically limited the right of states to use a different set of procedures for forensic patients, the resulting changes have produced a number of proposals that would continue the use of a separate set of procedures for this class of persons. Therefore, in analyzing issues related to forensic services, it is important to remember that no procedure should deny a forensic patient the same rights permitted to anyone else in the criminal justice system. He or she should also be provided appropriate mental health evaluation and necessary treatment in accordance with mental health statutes.

Forensic Evaluations

GENERAL GUIDELINES

There is a major distinction between a mental health professional providing direct service to a client and one providing forensic *evaluation* services. In performing forensic evaluations, the professional is not providing a direct service to a client but is providing a service to a third party, such as a court. Because of this third-party relationship, it is imperative that the professional clearly inform the criminal defendant of the purpose of the evaluation and to whom the results will be reported.[1] Therefore, the concepts of confidentiality and privilege cannot be applied in the same manner to information received from or about a forensic patient. In fact, the basis for the evaluation is usually a court order requiring the evaluation to take place.

COMPETENCY TO STAND TRIAL

Competency to stand trial is a legal issue, not a clinical or medical one. The concept is based on the Fifth and Sixth Amendments to the United States Constitution. The Fifth Amendment protects an individual from deprivation of liberty without due process of law; the Sixth Amendment specifies the rights of an individual in a criminal prosecution, including the right to be informed about the nature and consequences of the accusation. If a person's mental condition prevents him from understanding the charges against him or from participating in his own defense, then he is incompetent to stand trial.

The specific criteria to be used by courts in determining competency to stand trial include: an understanding of the nature of the legal process; a recognition of the consequences that could result from the accusation; and the ability to assist counsel in defense of the accusation. Although the most frequent reason for raising the question of competency is mental illness, other possibilities include mental retardation, physical impairment (such as deafness) and physical illness. Since the defendant must be competent in order to receive a fair trial, the judge and prosecutor, as well as the defense attorney, have a duty to raise questions about the possible incompetency of a defendant. Once the issue is raised and the judge determines that there is sufficient cause to question a defendant's competency, he must order an evaluation by an appropriate professional and make a finding after the evaluation.

Until recently, only psychiatrists were considered qualified to perform competency evaluations. Since there are only a limited number of psychiatrists available in the state systems, this requirement often resulted in prolonged inpatient evaluation in a large, centralized facility. However, in conjunction with other changes, many states now recognize that other professionals such as psychologists, social workers, and psychiatric nurses can perform these evaluations. Where such professionals are recognized, outpatient evaluations are more likely to be available to the courts.

One of the first comprehensive studies regarding the process of determining competency to stand trial was reported in a 1973 National Institute of Mental Health monograph entitled *Competency to Stand Trial and Mental Illness*. The principal investigator in the five-year study was Dr. Louis McGarry. Because irrelevant medical criteria had been applied by the psychiatric profession to the issue of competency, this study was designed to develop, validate, and demonstrate quantifiable clinical criteria to assess competency. For example, many psychiatrists would report to the court that a defendant was "psychotic" or "schizophrenic," or would use other psychiatric labels that did not assist the court in determining competency. This study also demonstrated that the courts themselves often confused the criteria for competency with the separate and different legal criteria for criminal responsibility. The result of the misunderstanding surrounding this issue was prolonged inpatient evaluation, even for defendants who were ultimately found to be competent.

The study demonstrated that evaluation for competency could be successfully performed on an outpatient basis by a variety of mental health professionals. If such screening determined the need for further evaluations, then an intensive and prolonged inpatient evaluation could be ordered. As a result, McGarry and his staff designed the Competency Assessment Instrument to help mental health professionals make evaluations by listing the pertinent legal issues involved. In addition to being tested in Massachusetts, this instrument has been used extensively in Tennessee, North Carolina, and Ohio.

There are other advantages to the use of outpatient evaluations for pretrial determinations of competency to stand trial. Frequently, a defendant's condition does not warrant hospitalization in order to make the competency decision, particularly if the professional performing the evaluation can adequately separate the clinical issues from the legal issue of competency. When only inpatient evaluations are available, an increased amount of time is required to complete the evaluation, and the evaluation can therefore delay trial. Also, when no outpatient services are available, there are limited support services for a defendant who is returned to jail. Finally, an inpatient hospitalization, even for evaluation, tends to label a defendant as mentally ill or criminally insane and may make it more difficult to refute the criminal charges.

CRIMINAL RESPONSIBILITY (INSANITY DEFENSE)

While competency to stand trial relates to the mental condition of the defendant at the time he is evaluated, the issue of criminal responsibility, or the defense of not guilty by reason of insanity (NGRI), relates back to the mental condition of the defendant at the time of the crime of which he is accused. Additionally, the legal standard is different and varies from state to state. A defendant must be competent to stand trial before he can use the defense of NGRI.

The evaluation for criminal responsibility is frequently ordered at the same time as the one for competency to stand trial. The evaluation is conducted in a similar manner and by the same mental health professionals. However, some states, such as Tennessee, permit only psychiatrists or licensed clinical psychologists to perform criminal responsibility evaluations, although a variety of master's level mental health professionals are recognized as able to perform competency evaluations.

The insanity defense is a concept that has long been a part of the common law, the English law from which our law evolved. The doctrine of *mens rea* first entered the English legal system more than eight centuries ago.[2] This doctrine states that the ability to form criminal intent is an inherent element of any offense. The intent to commit a crime is a critical element in proving a person guilty; the insanity defense is thus based on the theory that if a person's mental condition prevents him from forming the intent to commit a crime, he cannot be found guilty of the crime.

The insanity defense *per se* was first recognized by the courts in England in an 1843 murder case involving Daniel M'Naghten.[3] The standard known as the M'Naghten Rule, which evolved from this case, relieves a person from responsibility for his acts if he was laboring under such a defect of reason—from disease of the mind—as not to know the nature and quality of the act he was doing, or if he did know it, that he did not know that what he was doing was wrong.

The insanity defense has evolved in the law of all states, and most states still use a modified version of the M'Naghten Rule. However, there has been criticism about the outdated wording of the rule. A number of states have adopted the standard proposed by the American Law Institute: that a person is not responsible for criminal conduct if at the time of such conduct, as a result of mental disease or defect, he lacks substantial capacity either to appreciate the wrongfulness of his conduct or to conform his conduct to the requirements of the law. The terms *mental disease* and *defect* do not include an abnormality manifested only by repeated criminal or otherwise antisocial conduct.[4]

Mental Health Services to Persons Convicted of Crimes

A defendant convicted of a crime is usually placed in a correctional facility. An inmate may be mentally ill at the time of his conviction, or he may develop mental illness during incarceration. Although mental health services for inmates are frequently inadequate, most states have some services available. Some states refer all mental health problems to a central facility operated by the Department of Corrections or the Department of Mental Health. Others provide mental health services within the facility and utilize a unit within the institution when an inmate's condition requires segregation. Some authorities believe it is harmful to isolate mentally ill inmates from the general prison population. Such authorities also observe that the large facilities used for segregation have been greatly abused, with disruptive, aggressive, but nonpsychotic inmates becoming administratively defined as mentally ill.[5]

Until a 1965 United States Supreme Court decision, once an inmate was labeled mentally ill, particularly if he had been transferred to a segregated treatment facility, it was accepted practice for him to be denied parole hearings or even to be held beyond the expiration of his sentence. However, in *Baxstrom v. Herold*, the Supreme Court struck down this practice and asserted that a mentally ill prisoner cannot be held beyond the expiration of his term unless he is civilly committed to a mental health facility.[6] Additionally, the Court later held, in *Vitek v. Jones*,[7] that an inmate cannot be transferred to a mental health facility against his will without a hearing. This issue is discussed in more detail in the next section.

Some states, such as California, statutorily provide for commitments directly to facilities other than correctional institutions immediately after conviction.[8] Other states label groups convicted of certain crimes, such as sex offenders, and maintain certain evaluation requirements, but do not otherwise refer them to the Department of Mental Health unless they are also clinically evaluated to be mentally ill.[9] However, special services may be provided within the Department of Corrections based on the nature of the crime. The philosophy for establishing separate categories, such as sexual offenders, and treating them differently based on the nature of the crime was developed in the 1950s. Since that time, however, the process of evaluation, treatment, and detention of the mentally ill has changed dramatically.

Many professionals now question whether the commitment of a convicted defendant to a mental health facility based on a label related to the criminal conviction (ie, sex offender or drug abuser) rather than the person's mental condition can fulfill either a mental health goal or a correctional goal.[10] In states where such commitment is authorized, if a prisoner is in fact not mentally ill, he may still be hospitalized based on the type of crime he committed. Even if the person committed to the mental health facility is actually mentally ill, the correctional goal and the mental health goal may be entwined in such a manner as to be confusing to the public, the person so committed, and the treating facility. This is particularly true when the person is given an "indefinite" *sentence* to a treatment facility with release based on response to "treatment." Some experts have concluded that the best approach would be to abolish the quasi-criminal status, classify all persons convicted and sentenced as prisoners, and provide services to those who are mentally ill.[11]

"Criminal" Commitments

TREATMENT OF FORENSIC PATIENTS

Introduction. Once a person involved in the criminal justice system is evaluated and found to be mentally ill and in need of treatment, the manner in which the person may be committed and treated depends on his legal category. As stated previously, it has only been since recent United States Supreme Court decisions that forensic patients have been provided the same due process protections as civil patients who are judicially committed. However, in some instances the commitment procedures used for forensic patients still vary from civil commitments, and therefore these procedures are discussed as separate categories.

INCOMPETENT DEFENDANTS

The greatest changes produced by judicial decisions in forensics have occurred in the area of long-term commitment. Previously, a pretrial defendant found incompetent to stand trial would be committed indefinitely to a maximum-security facility based solely on his incompetency. The commitment lasted until he became competent. Therefore, defendants who had been found neither guilty of a crime nor mentally ill under civil commitment standards were frequently detained for longer periods than if they had actually been found guilty of the crime of which they were accused.[12]

In 1972 in *Jackson v. Indiana*, the United States Supreme Court ruled that a defendant could not be detained indefinitely in a mental hospital based solely on his incompetency to stand trial.[13] Theon Jackson was a mentally retarded deaf mute with limited ability to communicate. He was found to be incompetent to stand trial on two counts of robbery involving a total of nine dollars; and because his condition would not change, he would never become competent. At the time of the Supreme Court hearing, he had been detained three and one-half years. Since Indiana law required an incompetent defendant to be detained in a mental hospital until he became competent, Mr. Jackson had effectively received a life sentence.

The major impact of this decision was to mandate that the hospitalization of pretrial defendants be limited to a reasonable period of time for the purposes of assessing competency to stand trial and treating incompetents to help them become competent. However, the Court held that if a defendant is not likely to become competent in the foreseeable future, he must be either committed based on the same standards used for civilly committed patients or released from detention. The Supreme Court did not define "reasonable time" but found that the three and one-half years Jackson had been held was too long.

Most states had statutes similar to Indiana's and were faced with the mandate to change. One state, Tennessee, decentralized its forensic services to provide outpatient evaluations for pretrial defendants whenever possible.[14] If inpatient evaluation or treatment is required, the court may order thirty days' hospitalization. However, after that period, a defendant must be civilly committed in order to be detained further in the hospital.[15] Other states have continued to use different commitment standards for periods less than three and one-half years, or they have related the length of commitment to the length of the sentence for the crime of which the defendant has been accused but not convicted.[16]

Some commentators have speculated that the *Jackson* decision has produced a dilemma for several states because of the number of defendants who are incompetent but do not meet civil commitment standards. Therefore they cannot be detained in a mental hospital or proceed to trial and consequently must be released.[17] However, statistics from Tennessee, a state that has developed a comprehensive pretrial evaluation system that also provides support services in the jails, dispute this. In 1981, 1797 defendants were evaluated on an outpatient basis; only 289 of these were referred for inpatient evaluation, and of these, only 21 were civilly committed because they were incompetent to stand trial.[18] An uncertain but small number of defendants were found to be incompetent but not committable.

PERSONS FOUND NOT GUILTY BY REASON OF INSANITY

Procedures for placement of a defendant found not guilty by reason of insanity (NGRI) vary from state to state. Prior to the recent changes in mental health laws, these persons were automatically committed to a mental health facility without regard for their existing mental condition at the time of commitment. If the person was found to be no longer dangerous, release had to be ordered by the criminal court.[19]

There has been increased recognition that a person found NGRI may not be currently mentally ill or in need of hospitalization. Legally, a person found NGRI is not guilty of the crime; therefore, this person cannot be sent to prison to receive punishment. However, the procedure of automatic and indefinite detention in a hospital provides a similar alternative under the guise of providing treatment.

The legal system has now recognized that continued hospitalization should be related to the person's current mental condition—not his mental condition at the time of the crime.[20] However, there is still disagreement among courts in various jurisdictions as to whether an NGRI patient can be treated differently from a civil patient. Some courts have held that an NGRI can be held for a short period of evaluation regardless of mental condition, but for long-term hospitalization, he must be civilly committed in the same manner as any other person.[21] Other courts have ruled that a different standard of commitment can be used.[22] It will be up to the United States Supreme Court to determine whether or not it is denial of equal protection for a person found NGRI to be committed in a different manner from a civil patient.

In regard to the release of an NGRI from the hospital, some states still require court approval, while others permit the hospital to make the release decision. Unlike with the issue of commitment, most courts have agreed that it is constitutionally permissible to use a more stringent release standard for people who have been found NGRI than for other committed patients.[23] However, there is some disagreement regarding the standard to be used.

PERSONS CONVICTED OF CRIMES

The final category of commitment concerns persons convicted of crimes and sent to prison. As discussed previously, an inmate may be transferred to a mental health facility during his imprisonment. However, he cannot be transferred against his will unless adequate due process procedures are provided. The Court in *Vitek v. Jones* stated:

> Involuntary commitment to a mental hospital is not within the range of conditions of confinement to which a prison sentence subjects an individual. While a conviction and sentence extinguish an individual's right to freedom from confinement for the term of his sentence, they do not authorize the State to classify him as mentally ill and to subject him to involuntary psychiatric treatment without affording him additional due process protections. Here, the stigmatizing consequences of a transfer to a

mental hospital for involuntary psychiatric treatment, coupled with the subjection of the prisoner to mandatory behavior modification as a treatment for mental illness, constitute the kind of deprivations of liberty that require procedural protections.[24]

The only way a prisoner can be held beyond the expiration of his sentence owing to mental illness is by civil commitment to a mental health facility.[25]

Emerging Issues

In the past ten years, new procedures have been proposed in the forensic area. These proposals focus primarily on the use of the insanity defense. Several experts have taken the position that the insanity defense is abused and that psychiatry should not be involved in the criminal justice system.[26] They have proposed that the insanity defense therefore be abolished. However, there is a serious legal question whether or not this would be unconstitutional.

The United States Supreme Court has not ruled on the issue of abolishing the insanity defense. However, two state courts have reviewed the issue. The dates of these court cases indicate that the idea of abolishing the insanity defense is not, in fact, new. The Washington legislature attempted to abolish the insanity defense in 1910, but the Supreme Court of Washington declared the legislative action to be unconstitutional and restored the use of the insanity defense.[27] Later in the century, in 1931, Mississippi also attempted to abolish the insanity defense; again, the State Supreme Court declared the action to be unconstitutional.[28]

As discussed earlier in this chapter, the insanity defense is a concept deeply rooted in our legal history, along with the requirement of *mens rea*, or intent, for a criminal act. United States Supreme Court decisions in other areas regarding the requirement of intent to prove criminal conduct imply that the Court might not permit abolition of the insanity defense.[29] Also, the weight of scholarly opinion favors its retention.[30]

Over the years there have been several other recommendations to limit but not abolish the insanity defense. One of these recommendations is the use of a bifurcated trial procedure for a defendant who relies on the insanity defense. California first adopted the procedure in 1927.[31] Under this procedure, there are two trials; the first determines whether a criminal act was committed and, if so, whether the accused committed the act. If the accused is found guilty, a second trial is held for the sole purpose of determining whether the accused was insane at the time he committed the criminal act.

This legislation was designed to separate the element of intent from the question of guilt, thereby delaying the issue of intent until the second trial. The attempt has not been entirely successful, however. The California courts have allowed evidence of diminished capacity, a legal defense related to the issue of intent, to be used during the first trial.[32] Although several states have tried this concept, as of February 1978 only California, Colorado, and Wisconsin have retained the bifurcated system. All three states permit the issue of intent to be introduced at the first trial.[33]

The Supreme Courts of Arizona, Florida, and Wyoming have declared the bifurcated trial system unconstitutional.[34] The Florida Supreme Court stated:

> The principal issue presented for our consideration is whether the bifurcated trial system established by statute for the adjudication of guilt and insanity in criminal trial denies a defendant his right to due process of law under the state and federal constitutions. We . . . hold . . . that procedure unconstitutional.[35]

Therefore, there are actually no states that currently provide for a pure bifurcated trial procedure. Those states that began with such systems either modified them by legislative amendment or court decision to cure the constitutional imperfections, repealed the procedure, or declared it unconstitutional. The bifurcated system, at least as it was originally envisioned, has been destroyed. In order to correct the unconstitutional aspects of the procedure, it has been altered to admit the very evidence the system was originally designed to restrict.[36]

Perhaps as the result of the failure of these past efforts to limit the use of the insanity defense, a proposal has now emerged to add the plea of "Guilty But Mentally Ill" (GBMI). This concept was first adopted in Michigan; other states that have followed include Indiana, Illinois, and Georgia.[37]

One of the reasons there has been a popular push for the "GBMI" legislation is the misperception that such legislation abolishes the insanity defense. In fact, the legislation leaves the plea of NGRI as it stands; the proposed plea of GBMI would be available to defendants who have already pleaded NGRI but were, in fact, found guilty. The original proponents speculated that the GBMI plea would provide a jury with an option, thereby reducing the number of successful insanity defenses. However, in Michigan the statistics show the opposite result.[38] In a six-month period in 1975, Michigan had performed 92 insanity defense evaluations, of which 15 defendants were found insane. In a comparable six-month period in 1979, after implementation of the GBMI legislation, 589 evaluations for insanity defense were performed, and 50 defendants were found to be not guilty by reason of insanity.

Because the GBMI classification introduces new issues related to mental illness and criminal responsibility, there has been an increase in the number of defendants requesting, and attempting to use in their defense, pretrial psychiatric evaluations. The most obvious contradiction of the concept of guilty but mentally ill and its application is the reliance on *past* mental condition (at the time of the crime) for *present* treatment. If someone who pleads GBMI goes to prison, he receives treatment priority over a prisoner who developed mental illness in prison or did not plead GBMI. Otherwise, the legislation produces little change, since most states are required to provide mental health services to prisoners.

Perhaps the real intent behind this legislation can be identified in the provisions that place extra evaluation requirements on an individual pleading GBMI. For example, a GBMI inmate who is given probation must remain on probation no less than five years; a GBMI inmate cannot be released without psychiatric evaluation, even if he would otherwise be eligible for parole. It would appear that the reason for this legislation is the continued fear that there are large numbers of persons, both mentally ill and criminal, who are particularly dangerous and must have special treatment.

Another issue that developed in the 1970s was the application of the right to treatment in a forensic setting. The case that was extensively considered regarding this issue was *Davis v. Watkins*.[39] The court reviewed the care provided at Lima State Hospital in Ohio and mandated that treatment programs be initiated.

One additional issue that has been raised relates to the provision of expert testimony and is reviewed in *Estelle v. Smith*.[40] This case involved a pretrial psychiatric evaluation to determine the competency of a defendant to stand trial on the charge of first degree murder in which the state intended to seek the death penalty. After conviction, the same psychiatrist who had evaluated the defendant for competency testified on the issue of dangerousness to society at the sentencing hearing. Since the state used as evidence against the defendant the details of disclosures made during the pretrial psychiatric evaluation, the court held that it violated the defendant's Fifth Amendment privilege against self-incrimination. The case implies that if a pretrial evaluation is limited to determination of competence and insanity and is not used as evidence against a defendant—other than in relation to the insanity defense—a defendant does not have a constitutional right against self-incrimination.

Nursing Implications. The best policy for a nurse providing pretrial evaluation is to limit herself to an evaluation of the person's condition or competency. Also, if an expert reports an evaluation as a friend of the court, she is less likely to be viewed as an adversary of the defendant.

Conclusion

This chapter reviews the issues related to the provision of forensic services. The main goals in providing these services are to assist the courts with pretrial evaluations and to provide support services to mentally ill persons charged with or convicted of a crime so that their charges can be resolved fairly and in a manner similar to that used for other defendants. The evaluator's role is normally that of a friend of the court.

The criminal justice system has been forced to become more directly involved with more mentally ill defendants for a number of reasons. First, modern technology has permitted a large number of persons to be treated in the community rather than be institutionalized. Second, traditionally, pretrial defendants who were mentally ill were automatically detained in mental hospitals, and the courts were rarely confronted with final disposition of these defendants. Finally, if a defendant was found NGRI, he was automatically detained indefinitely. Now the courts are required to deal on an individual basis with these defendants.

The lawyers and judges involved in the criminal justice system frequently do not understand mental illness, however, and are hesitant to deal with the mentally ill defendant. Although court decisions now permit mentally ill defendants to proceed to trial and not be detained indefinitely without a proper hearing, there are new recommendations being made that would once again permit the indefinite incarceration of mentally ill defendants. Only the United States Supreme Court can resolve this issue.

Any recommendation that proposes to treat the mentally ill defendant or prisoner in a manner that deviates from the regular procedures should be suspect.[41] History demonstrates extensive abuse when deviation from the use of regular procedures is permitted.[42]

We are still faced with the unpopularity of the mentally ill defendant within the criminal justice system and among the public at large. Hopefully, rationality and basic legal principles will prevail in this atmosphere, particularly in the aftermath of the John Hinkley acquittal for his attempt on the life of a United States president.

REFERENCES

1. Jonas Rappeport: Forensic and General Psychiatry. American Journal of Psychiatry, 139:331-334, March 1982, at p. 332.
2. Paul S. Appelbaum: The Insanity Defense. Law and Psychiatry, 33(1):13-14, January 1982.
3. Ibid.
4. *Graham v. State of Tennessee,* 547 S.W. 2nd 531 (Tenn. 1977).
5. Loren H. Roth: Correctional Psychiatry. In William J. Curran (ed.): Modern Legal Medicine, Psychiatry and Forensic Science. Philadelphia, F.A. Davis Co., 1980, pp. 682, 687.
6. *Baxtrom v. Herold,* 383 U.S. 107 (1965).
7. *Vitek v. Jones*, 445 U.S. 480 (1980).
8. *California v. Ginese*, 175 Cal. Rptr. 383 (Cal. Ct. App. 1981).
9. Tennessee Code Annotated, sections 33-1301 through 33-1305.
10. Roth: Correctional Psychology, p. 679.
11. National Institute of Mental Health: Mental Health and Law: A System in Transition. Crime and Delinquency Issues Monograph Series; DHEW Publication No. (ADM) 75-176. Washington, DC, US Government Printing Office, 1973, p. 192.
12. James S. Walach: The Incompetency Plea: Abuses and Reforms. The Journal of Psychiatry and Law, 8(3):318-319; Joyce K. Laben and Lona D. Spencer: Decentralization of Forensic Services. Community Mental Health Journal, 12(4): 405-414, 1976.
13. *Jackson v. Indiana,* 406 U.S. 715 (1972).
14. Tennessee Code Annotated, section 33-708(a); Joyce K. Laben, Mark Kashgarian, Donald B. Nessa, and Lona D. Spencer: Reform From the Inside: Mental Health Center Evaluation of Competency to Stand Trial. Journal of Community Psychology, 5:52-62, 1977.
15. Tennessee Code Annotated, section 33-708(b).
16. Ronald Roesch and Stephen C. Coldberg: Treatment and Disposition of Defendants Found Incompetent to Stand Trial: A Review and a Proposal. International Journal of Law and Psychiatry, 2:349-370, 1979.

17. Ralph Slovenko: The Developing Law on Competency to Stand Trial. Journal of Psychiatry and Law, 5(2):165–200, Summer 1977.
18. Tennessee Department of Mental Health and Mental Retardation: Management Information System, Marthagem Whitlock, Director of Specialized Services.
19. Abraham S. Goldstein: Insanity Defense. New Haven and London, Yale University Press, 1967.
20. *Powell v. Florida,* 579 F2nd 324 (5th Cir. 1978). Also, *Benham et al., v. Edwards et al.,* No-80-9052 (No. Dist of Ga., May 27, 1982).
21. *United States v. Cohen,* No-80-00382 (D.C. Cir., March 5, 1982).
22. *Pohley v. Psychiatric Security Review Board,* 632 P2nd 15 (Or Ct. App. 1981). Also, *Colorado v. Chavez,* 629 P2d 1040 (Colo. Sup. Ct., 1978).
23. *Illinois v. Valdez,* No 52368, 52472 Cons. (Ill. Sup. Ct. Nov. 1979).
24. *Vitek v. Jones,* 445 U.S. 480 (1980).
25. *Baxtrom v. Herold,* 383 U.S. 107 (1965).
26. Richard A. Pasework and Mark O. Pasework: Cuckoo's Nest. Journal of Psychiatry and Law, 6:481-498, Winter 1978.
27. *State v. Strasberg,* 60 Wash. 106 at 1020 (1910).
28. *Sinclair v. State,* 161 Miss. 142, 132 So. 581 (1931).
29. *Palko v. Connecticut,* 302 U.S. 319 (1937); Also, *Wolf v. Colorado,* 338 U.S. 25 (1949).
30. The Insanity Defense. Should It Be Abolished. Newsweek, May 24, 1982, p. 61.
31. California Penal Code, Section 1026.
32. *People v. Corshem,* 51 Col. 2d 716, 337 P 2d 492 (1959). Also, *People v. Wells,* 33 Cal. 2d 330, 202 P 2d 53 (1949).
33. Susan Moseley: The Insanity Defense: An Old Procedure Under New Attack. Vanderbilt University School of Law, May 1979.
34. Ibid.
35. *State ex Rel Boyd v. Green,* 335 So. 2d 789 (Fla. 1978), p. 790.
36. Susan Moseley: The Insanity Defense, p. 18.
37. Michigan Code Annotated, Section 28, 1059.
38. Michael L. Cross and Robert D. Racine: Impact of Change in Legal Standard For Those Adjudicated Not Guilty By Reason of Insanity. Michigan, Center for Forensic Psychiatry, 1980.
39. *Davis v. Watkins,* 384 F Supp 1196 (N.D. Ohio 1974). Also, *Davis v. Balson,* 461 F Supp 842 (N.D. Ohio 1978).
40. *Estelle v. Smith,* 41 L.W. 4492 (1981).
41. National Institute of Mental Health: Mental Health and Law, p. 192.
42. Wendell R. Rals: Cold Storage. New York, Simon and Schuster, 1980.

CHAPTER 7
The Rights of Children

In most states, for most purposes, a juvenile or minor is defined as any individual younger than the age of eighteen.[1] The minor is presumed incompetent to make most decisions for himself, and the parent is the legally appropriate person to provide legal consent for actions affecting the juvenile. For example, a minor is not legally competent to execute a will, sign a contract, or consent to medical treatment. Nor does he have the right to engage in certain activities, such as voting, even with the consent of the parent. Some states have raised the age at which the purchase of beer or liquor is permitted to above eighteen.[2]

There are, however, exceptions to the presumed legal incompetence of a juvenile. Some states have statutes that specify exceptions and permit juveniles to act in their own behalf in certain areas. Exceptions include the right to seek treatment for drug abuse, the right to consent to contraception, and the right to seek psychiatric treatment.[3] However, states vary in the number of and the age requirements for the exceptions.[4] Also, a legal exception for one issue does not extend to other issues related to the juvenile.[5]

In addition to the statutory exceptions regarding the legal incompetence of juveniles, other factors may change the age at which a juvenile may act in his own behalf. These factors include marriage, emancipation, pregnancy, and parenthood.[6]

Emancipation is the oldest concept that recognizes circumstances under which the child-parent relationship can be severed prior to the child obtaining the age of majority. The more recent application of this doctrine has been a recognition that modern society makes children grow up faster; this has resulted in legislation in some states to provide mature minors with some recourse for obtaining legal recognition as adults.[7] The doctrine of emancipation permits a minor to assume the rights and responsibilities of adulthood regardless of age.[8] Emancipation may occur as a result of a judicial decree or automatically as a result of a statute.

Historically, the common-law doctrine of emancipation developed primarily to benefit parents and to provide a way for them to relinquish, expressly or implicitly, control of minor children. When this control is relinquished, the minor is required to function as an adult, and the parent is relieved of support obligation. On the other hand, emancipation may also occur when a parent deserts the minor or is guilty of nonsupport. The common-law emancipation is conditioned on an act or omission of the parent.[9] The exceptions are emancipation by marriage or service in the armed forces. However, normally the minor needs the parent's consent for either of these to occur.

Common-law emancipation did little to resolve conflicts between parent and child. Fourteen states now have laws that permit any minor seeking adult status to petition the court and, if he meets the criteria, to be granted adult status.[10] Although some of the statutes were enacted in past years based on common-law emancipation, later ones were designed to promote the independence of minors who demonstrate maturity. In addition, even if a juvenile is emancipated, his minority status may still be preserved for some purposes. For example, some states still require parental consent for general medical treatment even if a juvenile is married or emancipated.[11]

Until the litigation of the past two decades, the issues related to children centered on the ability of juveniles to consent or to act in their own behalf. However, the legal activity during this time has increasingly focused on efforts to "define, expand, and enforce their rights both in relation to families and in relation to broader social systems."[12] The result of the litigation has been to raise questions and change laws in new areas regarding the rights of juveniles.

Litigation concerning the rights of children in relation to their families can be divided into four areas[13]: (1) when children should have access to independent legal representation; (2) when the grounds are appropriate for removing children from their families and granting termination rights of parents to children; (3) when parental decisions about children should be reviewed by the court; and (4) when juveniles should be permitted to make decisions independent of parents.

All four categories can potentially affect the services provided by mental health professionals. Professionals are involved not only in providing direct services to juveniles, but also in providing indirect services by participating in evaluation of parents and in reporting to courts when custody or neglect are at issue. Categories (1) and (2) apply to these issues. Categories (3) and (4) more directly affect the day-to-day treatment provided by mental health professionals to minors, because they specify when a parent may consent to psychiatric treatment for a child, regardless of how the child feels, and when a child may consent to his own psychiatric treatment, regardless of his parent's position.

One of the most controversial issues reviewed by the courts is the right of parents in most states to commit their children for treatment at inpatient psychiatric facilities voluntarily. In this situation, unlike an adult, the juvenile does not have a right to a court hearing if he objects to his hospitalization. Neither in most states does he have the right to request his own release. In the 1970s, a number of lawsuits based on this practice were filed. They argued that the practice was unconstitutional, and that a court hearing should always be held to determine whether or not a juvenile should be committed. Subsequently, some states amended their statutes to provide more rights to juveniles in the admission process to psychiatric hospitals. For example, Tennessee amended its statute to permit juveniles older than 16 to admit themselves to psychiatric hospitals voluntarily, and it authorized juveniles of all ages to request their own release.[14]

This issue was finally reviewed by the United States Supreme Court in *Parham v J.L. & J.R.*[15] In this case, the Supreme Court held that a formal court hearing is not required to determine whether a minor can be voluntarily admitted to a psychiatric facility. The Court upheld the rights of parents to admit their children to mental hospitals if a neutral physician agrees that the admission is appropriate.[16]

In addition to the rights of minors in relation to their families, attention has also been focused on the rights of children in relation to the social and legal systems.[17] One landmark case that sought to protect the rights of minors in regard to the juvenile justice system was *Application of Gault.*[18] Prior to this case, juveniles charged with a crime had not been provided the same rights as an adult charged with a crime. The theory behind this was that juvenile court was established to protect the best interest of the child, not to treat him as a criminal. However, if a child was found to be delinquent, the consequences could be incarceration for the rest of his minority. *Gault* held that a minor charged with being delinquent was entitled to representation by counsel and to certain other due process rights. The key focus of *Gault* and subsequent decisions was to extend due process rights afforded adult criminals without abolishing the special consideration provided to juveniles. This same theory has been applied to proceedings in noncourt settings and to conflicts between parents and children.[19]

Finally, there has been litigation to protect the interests of children in institutions. The cases dealt with abuses and excesses in juvenile detention centers as well as lack of proper care and treatment in institutions such as retardation facilities.[20] Class action lawsuits and individual lawsuits were included. While there has been no definitive court decision on this issue, it is clear that with few exceptions, juveniles have the same rights as adults, particularly with regard to the right to treatment. Additionally, a minor has a right to education while institutionalized.

Nursing Implications. When a psychiatric nurse is involved in treating a minor, it is important to determine if anyone other than the parent has the right to provide consent for treatment. Even if the state law recognizes the right of the minor to consent in certain situations, or even if the minor is emancipated, the parent may still have rights that have to be recognized. Therefore, the issue of consent should always be clarified and documented in the juvenile's record.

REFERENCES

1. Monroe E. Trout: When Can a Child Consent to Treatment? Legal Aspects of Medical Practice, September 1978, pp. 25–28.
2. Tennessee Code Annotated, section 57-5-301 (e).
3. Trout, When Can a Child Consent, pp. 25–28.
4. Ibid.
5. Ibid., p. 25.
6. Ibid.
7. USEMA, The Uncertain Status of the Emancipated Minor: Why We Need a Uniform Statutory Emancipation of Minors Act. University of San Francisco Law Review, vol. 15, Spring and Summer 1981, pp. 473–507.
8. Ibid., p. 476.
9. Ibid.
10. Ibid., p. 477.
11. Trout, When Can A Child Consent, p. 25.
12. Jane Knitzer: Children's Rights in the Family and Society: Dilemmas and Realities. American Journal of Orthopsychiatry, vol. 52, no. 3, July 1982, p. 481.
13. Ibid.
14. Tennessee Code Annotated, section 33-601.
15. *Parham v. J.L. & J.R.,* 442 U.S. 584 (1979).
16. Charles Lidz, et al.: The Rights of Juveniles in Voluntary Psychiatric Commitments: Some Empirical Observations. Bulletin of the AAPL, vol. III, no. 2, p. 169.
17. Knitzer, Children's Rights, p. 787.
18. *Application of Gault,* 407 P2d 760 (1965).
19. Knitzer, Children's Rights, p. 487.
20. Ibid., pp. 487–490.

CHAPTER 8
Malpractice Issues

Malpractice suits have greatly increased within the last few years, and the nurse working in a psychiatric setting now is more likely to be a defendant in a lawsuit than ever before. An individual who thinks he has been aggrieved by a nurse may bring suit in a state or federal court for monetary damages for alleged negligence. Negligence is a civil matter that comes within the purview of tort law. It is a dispute between two or more citizens or business entities in which one claims that the other breached a duty and caused damage.

Elements of Negligence

Before discussing cases that have been filed against professionals, such as nurses, for psychiatric care, it is important to review the elements of negligence as defined in a malpractice action. Malpractice is based on the fact that the public expects that the performance of a professional or specialist will measure up to the standards of the profession or specialty. A person avowing a professional status is held to the degree of skill claimed by that profession. Therefore, the test of fault or breach of duty in malpractice cases is determined not by reference to the traditional "reasonable and prudent man" standard used in ordinary personal injury cases, but by a standard that measures whether there was a departure from customary professional conduct. Thus, the legal standard of care for a nurse is that of a "reasonable and prudent" nurse.

It is the legal responsibility of health care givers to provide safe care.[1] Each individual who provides health care to an individual or family is personally responsible and liable for his or her own conduct. The professional nurse might also be responsible for other professionals through the supervisory process. When a person files a lawsuit against a professional person for malpractice, it must first be established that the professional owed a duty to the patient and, further, that his or her practice fell below a reasonable standard of care. Consequently, a nurse must apply the minimum standard of care in his or her practice that any other reasonably prudent nurse would apply in the same circumstances. Whether a nurse is employed by an agency or another individual or is self-employed in private practice, he or she has a legal duty to give safe and appropriate care to patients and families for whom responsibility is given. A causal link between the treatment or care provided by the nurse and the injury to the patient must also be established. The courts will look at the circumstances of particular events to determine whether it was foreseeable that the individual would be harmed as a result of the nurse's actions. The last element the plaintiff must prove is that an injury was suffered and damages resulted from the nurse's negligence.[2]

Even if a nurse has provided a high standard of care, defense against a possible malpractice action is dependent upon proper documentation that established procedures have been followed. It is important to document care provided in order to avoid malpractice suits.

Case Examples

ABILLE V. UNITED STATES OF AMERICA

The following is a case illustrating these legal concepts. Manuel Abille was 51 years old and had been taking the drug Reserpine for high blood pressure.[3] On April 15, 1977, a physician discontinued his use of this drug because the patient had developed depression, a side effect sometimes associated with Reserpine. There was no prior history of depression or suicidal tendencies. The patient voluntarily admitted himself to the United States Air Force Hospital at Elmendorf Air Force Base in Anchorage, Alaska, on April 26, 1977. The following day, he was seen by one of three psychiatrists on the hospital staff. The doctor noted that Mr. Abille had a flattened affect, suicidal ideation for a duration of three weeks, and sleep disturbances. His diagnosis was depressive neurosis, hypertension, and reactive depression to Reserpine.

Patients in this facility were assigned a particular status based upon their mental conditions. Mr. Abille was given an "S-1" status, which meant that he was not permitted to leave his psychiatric unit without a staff escort. There were no further notations by a physician in the record. On April 27, 1977, the nurse's notes stated that Mr. Abille had slept only three hours the preceding night. The following day it was observed and recorded that he had a brighter affect, and he commented that he wished to go home. On April 29 it was indicated that Mr. Abille had not slept well, was anxious, was less depressed, and was resisting group therapy. He further stated his desire to discuss his problems with the physician. On that day, a psychiatric technician wrote that Mr. Abille was depressed and expressed concern about his suicidal ideation. There were no further notes in the record.

On April 30 the psychiatric nurses assigned to the ward began permitting Mr. Abille the privilege of an "S-2" status, which meant that he could leave the unit escorted by a staff member or another patient who was permitted more freedom. Additionally, he could go unescorted to designated places within the hospital for specific purposes.

The government memorandum that described the privileges of an "S-2" patient stated that this level was assigned to individuals who had been in the hospital at least 24 hours, were not considered suicidal, or had not demonstrated behaviors that might indicate that the person would be harmful to himself or others. On this particular Saturday, Mr. Abille was allowed to go to mass unattended in the building. He returned without incident. He was then permitted to use a razor to shave and to go to breakfast without an escort. After he left the ward, he was found dead on the ground outside. He apparently leaped to his death from an unsupervised lounge on the seventh floor.

There was no written order by the physician to change Mr. Abille's status from "S-1" to "S-2." However, there was a change of status written by a nurse *after* Mr. Abille's death on a verbal order from the physician on April 29. The physician did not appear at the trial, and the court concluded that his answers to questions at a deposition about the change of status orders were not persuasive. It was concluded that no order had been written before the death occurred. The court stated that the nurses had been acting in good faith,

> but the defendant's nurses were acting below the standard of care when they permitted Abille to leave the ward unescorted while he was classified S-1, his status not having been changed by a physician. Inasmuch as he had been diagnosed to be suicidal, his suicide attempt was a foreseeable risk and must therefore be considered as a proximate result of the negligent act of the nurses.[4]

After Mr. Abille's death, the physician had written that the "symptoms of a suicidal disposition continued to be displayed by Abille and recognized by the staff." At the trial, an expert witness testified that risks vary from high to low in relation to suicidal patients. The concept of least restrictive alternative makes it difficult to assess the freedom to grant a patient based on his suicidal potential. The court concluded that the potential for committing suicide was a matter of judgment. However, the physician's failure to keep ongoing progress notes and the lack of a written order for reclassification did fall below the standard of care. The survivors who brought the suit were awarded monetary damages.

This case clearly illustrates that the nurses employed to care for psychiatric patients in this facility did have a legal duty to Mr. Abille. The care fell below the standard when no written order confirming the change of privilege status was placed in the record. Because he was a suicidal risk, it was foreseeable that with more freedom to move around, he might commit suicide. It was concluded that these acts were the proximate cause of Mr. Abille's death. Because there was a fatal injury, damages were awarded to the survivors.

RAY V. AMERI-CARE HOSPITAL

In a contrasting decision, another hospital was found to be not liable for a patient's suicide. Mr. Ray was admitted on January 14, 1976, with a diagnosis of paranoid schizophrenia. He seemed to do all right for a few hours after admission, but when a laboratory technician attempted to draw blood for tests, the patient had a physical reaction that necessitated the calling of the physician. Because of his psychotic symptoms, Mr. Ray was given Haldol, and his visitors were limited to the immediate family. He appeared to have a restful night but dozed infrequently. In the early morning hours on January 19, 1976, he was found drowned in the bathtub. The record showed that he had a delusion that he was able to breathe underwater. It had been concluded prior to his death that it would be to his detriment to be placed in a small room or to use mechanical restraints because of his paranoid symptoms.

The court concluded that it is not possible to take precautions for every delusion that a mentally ill person might experience, and that the physician did not fall below the standard of care in prescribing treatment for Mr. Ray.[5] It should be noted that each case will be determined by the individual facts. The courts will look to the behavior exhibited by the patient prior to the incident and to the professional's response to the symptomatology exhibited.

DELICATA V. BOURLESSES

In *Delicata v. Bourlesses*, the plaintiffs appealed a ruling by a medical malpractice tribunal who decided that the following facts did "not present a legitimate question of liability appropriate for judicial inquiry."[6] Carmela Delicata was 39 years of age and was suffering from cancer. She had several surgeries performed, but the cancer had metastasized to her bones. She began receiving chemotherapy.

In November 1975, she attempted suicide in the presence of her daughter. She was subsequently hospitalized in the psychiatric ward of New England Deaconess Hospital on November 17, 1975. On November 19, she expressed thoughts of suicide and asked the staff to "assist in this task of suicide."[7] She was seen by a staff psychiatrist and a psychologist, who both indicated that suicidal precautions and constant supervision were not necessary. However, she continued to be depressed, and on November 22 it was recommended by a staff psychiatrist that she begin electroconvulsive therapy in two days.

She was asked to discuss the therapy with her husband. She apparently did not want the ECT, and she was overheard by another patient who subsequently related to the staff that she told her husband she wanted to die. The husband became disgusted with her and left. Mrs. Delicata was last seen at 9:00 p.m., when she went to take a bath. Forty minutes later she was found fully clothed, submerged in a water-filled tub. She was resuscitated without success.

A nurse expert witness testified that based upon her examination of the patient's records, the patient should have been observed at least every fifteen minutes. She further testified that because the patient was not observed for a forty-minute period (which was unacceptable nursing practice), the nurse's negligence contributed to the cause of death.[8] The court subsequently ruled that

> despite the psychiatrist's finding three days before that suicidal precautions were unnecessary, a reasonably skillful nurse in the defendant's position, would at a minimum have monitored Mrs. Delicata during the bath, based on the patient's condition that evening, or should either have instituted closer supervision on her own initiative or sought permission from a staff physician to implement stricter controls.[9]

The court concluded that there was a legitimate question of liability and that further judicial inquiry was indicated. Irene Murchison comments in a book on legal aspects of nursing that "it is a significant legal decision to hold the nurse accountable for failure to use the knowledge and skills of a professional psychiatric nurse in developing and sustaining a plan of care based on continuing reassessment of patient needs."[10] It should be noted that the nurse was sued personally, an occurrence that is becoming more frequent.

Chapter Eight

Documentation

As illustrated by these case studies, an important aspect of care for the mental health client is an adequate documentation of the assessment, diagnosis, and treatment plans and care of the individual. Not only is this necessary as a record of care for the client, but it is also important in communicating with other personnel about the individual's prior and continuing care.

To characterize accurately the client's condition, a descriptive account utilizing the senses should be implemented: what is seen, what is heard, what is smelled, and what is felt (for example, skin temperature). Such accounts should describe therapeutic interventions undertaken.[11] Only the facts should be presented; conclusions should be left to the reader. When any question about the record is raised by the client, an attorney, or the courts, the record will probably be subpoenaed and examined. Records are important as an account of client care, and they also will be supportive to the nurse named a defendant in a lawsuit. Treatment plans should be supported in the record by noting their implementation. When treatment is not recorded, unless an extraordinary amount of evidence is presented to the contrary, it will probably be considered not to have been done.

The following facts describe a situation in which information was recorded but not communicated to law officers in the community as requested. Mr. Alonzo Bush was on parole in California when he sustained a severe head injury which necessitated brain surgery. Following this procedure, he was allowed to go to South Dakota by the California Parole Board. He was admitted to the Veterans Administration Hospital (V.A.) at Hot Springs, South Dakota, in September 1973. The symptoms listed by the admitting doctor included organic brain syndrome and a psychotic disorder. In the next two and a half years, Mr. Bush was admitted and discharged from V.A. hospitals 23 times.

In January 1975, while a patient at the V.A. Hospital in Hot Springs, Mr. Bush attacked another patient without provocation. The parole officer was called, and the sheriff apprehended Mr. Bush at the V.A. Hospital and incarcerated him. This information was included in the record. At the end of January, Mr. Bush transferred to an alcoholic treatment ward in Yankton, South Dakota. He was released from this program in March 1975.

He was later admitted to another V.A. facility at Fort Meade. During this stay he attacked a staff member, wrestling him to the ground. Because he had signed out against advice, he was escorted out of the hospital. He was returned to the hospital the next day, and the staff was instructed to notify the police upon his departure. There was much subsequent discussion among the treatment staff about what to do with Mr. Bush. It was finally decided that he did not meet commitment standards. Mr. Bush left the locked ward of the V.A. Hospital and was jailed by the sheriff. He attempted to set fire to the jail. Because they could not control him, he was returned to the hospital, again with instructions to contact law enforcement officials on his discharge.

Mr. Bush requested to be transferred from the locked ward to the alcoholic treatment ward. He was subsequently discharged from this program by a physician who had not thoroughly read the record. The law enforcement officials were not notified. Mr. Bush became embroiled in an altercation, pulled a revolver, and shot a man. A surviving relative of the victim filed a lawsuit against the federal government for wrongful death.

The court ruled that the hospital had been requested to notify the police upon Bush's release. This information was contained in the record. There was a failure on the part of the hospital to act responsibly, contributing substantially to the victim's death, and the hospital was found liable for the damages resulting from the wrongful death. This case illustrates the importance of being informed about a patient's history, of the critical issue of aftercare planning for such an individual, and of the imperative nature of good communication within an institutional system.

The Nurse as a Witness

There are two capacities in which a nurse might be called upon to testify, as a lay witness and as an expert witness at a hearing or trial. In situations in which the nurse is asked to testify as a lay witness, she will testify to the facts and be asked to describe what she observed, any communications to her, or information she might have overheard.[13] These data would come from the nurse's direct knowledge. An accurate recording of patient care and good observational skills will be helpful to a nurse in this situation.

When called upon as an expert witness, the nurse is permitted to give opinions. In matters defining the standard of care given by the nurse to psychiatric patients, the witness could be a psychiatric nurse defining the accepted practice. The nurse is an expert when the knowledge is specialized and when because of nursing experience, expertise, and information, she can define standards of practice. Preparation time for this endeavor can be lengthy. However, it is important that nurses provide this service to improve patient care. They also are the best evaluators of nursing care.

Recently, courts and authors have acknowledged that nurses are the experts concerning nursing care. W.T. Eccard states in a law review article that "allowing a physician to testify in nursing malpractice actions or a nurse to testify in medical malpractice actions simply because they share common areas of knowledge unnecessarily confuses the issue."[14]

Vicarious Liability

The concept of vicarious liability of a *respondeat superior* (let the master speak) is predicated on the employer's relationship with his employees.

It is the institution's responsibility to employ stable, knowledgeable people, and an institution can indeed be held liable for the misconduct and negligence of its employees. It is within the institution's purview both to begin and to terminate employment, as is the case with virtually any employer.

This accountability of the institution and its ability to absorb and spread the costs of any financial burden resulting from legal liability have largely precluded legal actions against individual nurses.

At one time, too, it was difficult to obtain financial remuneration from nurses sued individually because of the relatively low economic status of the profession. This situation gradually has changed, and lawsuits against individual nurses are being filed in increasing numbers.

Some nurses believe that as long as the employer is answerable for their conduct, individual responsibility is absolved. While it is true that an employer is held accountable for its employees, a nurse is always accountable for professional behavior in relation to client care.

In a landmark case, *Darling v. Charleston Community Memorial Hospital*, a hospital was held liable for not calling in consultants to help a physician care for a young man who had sustained a broken leg.[15] The nurses observed the steadily deteriorating condition of the man's leg and failed to report the situation to the hospital administration.

The court defined a new duty for the nurse, "that of informing the hospital administration of any deviation in proper medical care that poses a threat to the well-being of the patient."[16] Based on the bylaws of the hospital and the Standards for Hospital Accreditation promulgated by the Joint Commission on Accreditation of Hospitals, the hospital should have reviewed the work of the physician or required consultation when the patient failed to respond to treatment. It is therefore the duty of the nurse to report to the administration any situation in which a professional doctor or nurse is not administering the acceptable standard of care.

Other Standards of Care

Standards have been developed by the American Nurses' Association and other nursing organizations regarding the delivery of nursing care. The standards established by the Association, as well as those set by organizations coordinating Medicare and Medicaid payments, are in many cases higher than the minimum standards traditionally required by the courts. Because these standards are steadily being raised, in the future the courts may use these higher standards to determine liability.

REFERENCES

1. Mary D. Hemelt and Mary Ellen Mackert: Dynamics of Law in Nursing and Health Care, 2nd. ed. Reston, VA., Reston Publishing Co., 1982, p. 22.
2. Ibid.
3. *Abille v. United States of America,* 484 F.Supp. 703 (1980).
4. Ibid., p. 707.
5. *Ray v. Ameri-Care Hospital,* 400 So2d 1127 (1981).
6. *Delicata v. Bourlesses,* 404 N.E. 2nd 667 at 688 (1980).
7. Ibid., p. 669.
8. Ibid., p. 670.
9. Ibid., p. 671.
10. Irene Murchison, Thomas S. Nichols, and Rachel Hanson: Legal Accountability in the Nursing Process, 2nd ed. St. Louis, The C.V. Mosby Co., 1982, p. 168.
11. Hemelt and Mackert: Dynamics of Law, p. 178. Also, Alice Kerr: Nurses Notes, That's Where the Goodies Are! Nursing 75, February 1975, pp. 34–40.
12. *Williams v. United States of America,* 450 F.Supp. 1040 (S.D., 1978).
13. Murchison and Nichols: *Legal Accountability,* p. 106.
14. W.T. Eccard: Revolution in White—New Approaches in Treating Nurses as Professionals. Vanderbilt Law Review, 30:865, 1977.

15. *Darling v. Charleston Community Memorial Hospital,* 33 Ill. 2d 253, 211 N.E., 2d 253 (1966).
16. Irene Murchison and Thomas S. Nichols: Legal Foundations of Nursing Practice. New York, The Macmillan Company, 1970, p. 142.

CONCLUSION

Just as the concepts, theories, and practice of nursing are constantly evolving and changing, so are the legal issues related to the practice of mental health nursing. As discussed in the Introduction, changes in mental health law have been continuous and numerous during the 1970s and into the 1980s. Because of these changes, the nurse should be cognizant of the current status of the law related to mental health clinical practice. However, there is *no substitute for legal advice and counsel on specific issues from an attorney retained by the institution where the nurse is employed or retained individually by the nurse.*

It is hoped that the information in this book will stimulate nurses to review their own practices and to question those individuals who might violate patients' rights. Nurses traditionally have been advocates for quality health care but have often felt powerless to make changes due to lack of knowledge and political power. Since nurses are responsible for their own individual practices, keeping abreast of mental health law will enable the nurse to make informed judgments about practice in order to provide quality care to clients and insure them of their rights. As an outcome of this process, the nurse should feel a personal and professional satisfaction that has not been possible in the past.

Index

Addington v. Texas, 27
Admissions, (*see also* Commitment),
 adults, 22-28
 children, 79
 civil, 25-28
 emergency, 24-25
 indefinite, 25-28
 voluntary, 22-24
Advocacy, 41-42, 48

Baxstrom v. Herold, 66
Behavioral modification, 38-39

Children, rights of, 77-80
Commitment (*See* Admissions)
Community Mental Health Centers Act of 1963, 4
Competency,
 of the individual, 15-16, 23-24
 to stand trial, 62-64
Confidentiality, 7-8, 32, 62

Dangerousness, 26-27, 28
Darling v. Charleston Community Memorial Hospital, 88-89
Davis v. Balson, 32
Delicata v. Bourlesses, 84-85
Dix, Dorothea, 2-3
Dixon v. Weinberger, 21, 40
Documentation (*see also* Records), 28-29, 31, 33, 34, 55, 86-87

Estelle v. Smith, 72-73
Electroconvulsive therapy (ECT) (*see also* Rights of clients), 25, 45, 56-57
Emancipation, 77
Expert witness, 87-88

Forensics,
 competency to stand trial, 62-64
 criminal responsibility, 64-65
 evaluations, 62
 guilty but mentally ill (GBMI), 71-72
 incompetent defendants, 67-68
 insanity defense, 64-65
 M'Naghten Rule, 65
 not guilty by reason of insanity (NGRI), 68-69
 sexual offenders, 66

Forensics (continued),
   treatment of patients, 67-68

Guardianship, 15-16, 23, 47, 51, 52
Guilty but mentally ill (GBMI), 71-72

Historical trends, 1-6

Informed consent, 12-14, 23, 57
  nursing implications, 14-15

Jackson v. Indiana, 67-68
Juveniles (*see* Children)

Kaimowitz v. Department of Mental Health, 57-58

Least restrictive alternative, 21-22, 33, 36, 37, 40, 46, 49

Malpractice (*see* Negligence)
M'Naghten Rule (*see also* Forensics), 65
Medication, right to refuse (*see* Rights of Patients),

Negligence, 81-87
Not guilty by reason of insanity (NGRI), 68-69
Nursing implications,
  admissions, 28-29
  advocacy, 42
  behavioral modification, 39
  confidentiality, 12
  electroconvulsive therapy (ECT), 57
  guardianship, 15-16
  informed consent, 14-15
  power of attorney, 17
  pre-trial evaluation, 73
  psychosurgery, 58
  research on the mentally ill, 39-40
  right to refuse treatment, 55-56
  seclusion and restraints, 34
  treatment of children, 80

O'Connor v. Donaldson, 26-27, 37-38
Outpatient treatment, 17-18, 28-29

Parham v. J.L. & J.R., 79
Payment for hospitalization, 35

Power of attorney, 17
Privilege (*see also* Confidentiality), 7-8
Psychosurgery, 45, 57-58

Records,
  access to, 9, 32
  patients, 32, 86-87
  review of, 32-33
Release of information, 8-9
  court order, 8-9
  release form, 8
  subpoena, 8
Rennie v. Klein, 45-49, 50-52
Research on the mentally ill, 39-40
Right to aftercare, 40
Rights of patients,
  children, 77-80
  civil rights, 31-32
  to refuse treatment, 24, 45-58
  electroconvulsive therapy (ECT), 56-57
  medication, 45-56
  psychosurgery, 57-58
  to treatment, 35-38
Rogers v. Okin, 33, 49-54
Rouse v. Cameron, 35
Rush, Benjamin, 2

Seclusion and restraints, 33-34
Sexual offenders (*see* Forensics)

Tarasoff v. Regents of the University of California, 9-12
Treatment plan, 37

Vicarious viability (*respondeat superior*), 87-88
Vitek v. Jones, 66, 69-79

Work, inpatient, 34-35
Wyatt v. Stickney, 35-38

Youngberg v. Romeo, 27-28, 54-55

MEDICAL LIBRARY
ST. JOSEPH MERCY HOSPITAL
660 CLINTON STREET
DETROIT, MI 48226